ENGAGE
WITH
STORY

Turn every project into a success story — captivate stakeholders through powerful storytelling.

Abderrazak HAMZAOUI

DEDICATION

To my wife Fatima

To my daughter Salma

CONTENTS

ACKNOWLEDGMENTS

This book would never have come to life without the quiet presences, the words planted at just the right moment, the gestures made in the shadows. To all those who, near or far, extended a hand — whether through advice, a look, silence, or support — I offer my thanks. But not a mechanical thank you. A thank you that is alive, rooted in a deep recognition of connection.

To Ms. Linda Rising, first of all, whose foreword did more than simply open this book — it gifted it to the world with a special light, the light of authentic encouragement.

To Ms. Mounia Boucetta, a woman of commitment and intellectual grace, who, despite the rarity of her time, made space to write the preface. Her gesture was more than a signature — it was an act of trust.

To Ms. Carla Casséus, for her powerful testimonial, full of truth and vision, like a bridge reaching toward a more inclusive   future.

To Ms. Nadja El Fertasi, who took the time to read and honor this work with a comment that, to me, was more than praise — it was a compassionate mirror.

To Ms Sofia Lopez, whose constructive feedback did not take away from the text's strength but instead refined its soul.

And finally, there is Mr Nigel Thurlow. I could list his titles and credentials — but what stays with me most is the precision of his words, his deep encouragement, and those comments that echoed long after reading. Like a quiet promise: that what is created from the heart always finds its resonance.

FOREWORD

Abderrazak Hamzaoui in his new book, ENGAGE WITH STORY, is not just giving us a lot of valuable information about stories. He is using stories to teach us about stories! The stories he is using for this teaching adventure are especially compelling because they are personal. Nothing is more interesting to us than hearing what others have done, the challenges they have overcome and the lessons they have learned.

I have long been intrigued by the power of stories. As a technical person with a lot of technical training and education, I can remember in my younger days, relying on logical argument to convince friends, family, and colleagues. Sometimes I was successful, but when logic didn't work, I usually blamed the listener, thinking the other person was not very smart or didn't care or wasn't really listening. Of course, I never applied this logical conclusion to myself! It was only when I began to be interested in neuroscience that I learned that our brains are hardwired to not only love but also to be convinced by stories. Research with volunteers in imaging machines has shown that when hearing a logical argument our brains immediately begin to fight against what we are hearing and look for loopholes and flaws in the presentation. When we hear stories, however, our brains begin to "synch up," and not only pay attention to what the presenter is saying but eagerly wait for what will happen next. Stories are influential.

Scientists are now telling us that much of what we believe we see, hear, feel, and believe is based on a personal narrative that our brains create for us. We make it up as we go along and if new information doesn't fit, our brain editor will toss it out as irrelevant. We like a good story and base our entire lives on it. The world and our place in it must make "sense" to us and that means it must fit our story.

Stories likely appeared in our evolutionary history about the same time that our ancestors figured out what to do with fire. Fire not only allowed us to cook food and stay warm, it also extended the length of the day. It didn't provide a lot of light, so we were forced to gather around it when darkness descended and since we could do much else, we began to share stories. This feeling of being together, being just a little nervous in the dark, being dependent on the presence of others in our tribe, telling stories, is still with us today. It's not just children who love bedtime stories.

Out of this ancient environment, leaders of the tribe were born. They captured our attention with their tales of courage and decisiveness. They were our heroes. This is still true today. Leaders in organizations, in communities and in countries are story tellers. Some might call them salesmen or saleswomen. They spin a good yarn and we get caught up in it. We don't always do a good job of analyzing what they are saying. We are just captivated by them. It's called charisma. Great leaders have it. Obviously, this talent can be used for good or evil. History is full of examples of both.

Abderrazak Hamzaoui puts storytelling under the microscope. He analyzes the components and the styles. He has created templates to help us be better writers and tellers of stories. He focuses on the business environment. His example scenarios will be especially meaningful for those of you who already understand the power of stories and want concrete suggestions for making your stories better. There's not only good information here. There is wisdom. I know I learned a lot. You will, too.

Linda Rising

PREFACE

The art of storytelling has always been central to ancient civilizations — from Egyptian funerary texts and Homeric epics to Roman founding myths. These cultures grasped a profound truth: narratives do not merely recount events — they shape the world, transmit values, and forge collective memory.

In Arabo-Islamic civilization, quṣṣāṣ (storytellers) were present in mosques, public squares, and marketplaces, narrating prophetic tales, mystical journeys, and popular legends. One Thousand and One Nights (Alf Layla wa-Layla) stands as one of the greatest masterpieces of world storytelling — a powerful illustration of narrative as a means of survival and life-preserving act.

Today, storytelling remains a powerful tool for influence, persuasion, and human connection. It is employed across diverse fields such as marketing, politics, education, personal development, and diplomacy. In a world overwhelmed by information, stories offer structureotion, and meaning to otherwise raw, fragmented, and abundant data. As Maya Angelou once said, "People will forget what you said, people will forget what you did, but people will never forget how you made them feel."

Abderrazak Hamzaoui's book offers a compelling exploration of storytelling as a powerful tool for inspiration, mobilization, and transformation—particularly in an era marked by information saturation, unpredictability, and multifaceted challenges.

Hamzaoui's work is more than just a book — it is a journey through the many dimensions of storytelling. As you read it, his insights resonate deeply, inviting you to explore storytelling as a powerful and meaningful resource in both your professional practice and everyday life.

Mounia Boucetta

Senior Fellow at the Policy Center for the New South

Former State Secretary to the Minister of Foreign Affairs- Morocco-

TESTIMONIAL

Why Business Analysts Should Read This Book?

In today's volatile and high-stakes project environments, success isn't just about process—it's about connection, clarity, and adaptability. *A Tale That Transformed My Existence* is more than a book; it's a tactical guide for business analysts who want to drive value beyond expectations especially in complex, high-risk projects.

When projects are under pressure—tight timelines, conflicting interests, shifting scopes—success often hinges not just on process, but on how we communicate, engage, and influence. This book equips BAs with tools to turn ambiguity into clarity, resistance into alignment, and stakeholders into champions.

PART I – Story Power & Stakeholders Engagement

This section highlights how storytelling empowers business analysts to turn complex, high-risk projects into cohesive, goal-driven initiatives. It offers practical tools to map stakeholders, align visions, and prevent scope creep. By mastering narrative techniques, analysts can simplify complexity, gain stakeholder buy-in faster, and boost team engagement—key factors in delivering under pressure and within budget.

PART II – Project Process and Storytelling

This section links storytelling to each phase of project management, helping business analysts strengthen communication from initiation to closing. It shows how to use narrative to justify the business case, align teams during execution, and turn reports into impactful insights. Storytelling also helps close projects with a lasting narrative of success — boosting credibility and driving future improvements.

PART III – Tailoring Storytelling to Stakeholder Types

This section teaches business analysts how to tailor communication to different stakeholder types — crucial in high-risk projects with competing interests. It provides tools to engage, inform, and anticipate stakeholder behavior, helping prevent costly misalignment. The final chapter emphasizes using storytelling to bring clarity to complexity, enabling analysts to lead with purpose and deliver high-impact results with precision and control. Business analysts with narrative strategies to frame chaos into logic, allowing teams to act decisively even in uncertain environments.

Through clear, structured insights, *Prologue: A Tale That Transformed My Existence* offers more than a guide for business analysts — it's a powerful communication toolkit for any professional navigating high-stakes decisions. From aligning teams under pressure, to influencing stakeholders with purpose, to simplifying complexity, this book equips readers to drive results with clarity and empathy. Congratulations to the author for crafting a resource that not only strengthens storytelling and stakeholder engagement, but also empowers professionals across industries to lead conversations that end in win-win outcomes — whether in sales, negotiation, or collaboration.

Carla Casséus, Senior Business Analyst &

Founder of CC4 solutions,

Advocate for inclusive digital transformation

PROLOGUE: A TALE THAT TRANSFORMED MY EXISTENCE

Many years ago, Ahmed embarked on his professional journey as a fledgling engineer. He was confronted with the challenges of advocating for his unique ideas, seeking enhancement in both his professional and personal spheres, and molding his nascent identity. He grappled with these challenges through voracious reading and profound dialogues with peers. However, one persistent frustration eluded resolution: his fear of speaking in front of an attractive woman or a public audience.

At the beginning of a session on Chinese culture, in front of his colleagues and a communication expert who was there to enhance their skills in building partnerships with Chinese counterparts, Ahmed found himself hesitating to speak. The expert seemed unimpressed with the interventions from his colleagues. Ahmed was taken aback when the expert voiced the exact thoughts, he had struggled to articulate himself. His hesitation swiftly morphed into a profound sense of frustration.

A more daunting challenge arose during a communication workshop, a collaborative effort between his organization and the faculty of educational sciences. Each participant was required to prepare and deliver a presentation in front of their peers, captured on video for subsequent critique. As Ahmed watched the playback of his performance, he wished for the earth to swallow him whole. He would have traded anything to avoid watching himself present. The facilitator offered constructive remarks, yet Ahmed's mind lingered not on the feedback but on the facilitator's eloquent delivery. He admired it and yearned to emulate such grace. After the facilitator concluded his remarks and awaited a response, Ahmed posed a singular, impactful question: "What distinguishes your faculty from other teacher training institutions?"

"We cultivate educators who do not merely teach; they contemplate the very essence of education," the expert replied.

It was as though Ahmed had been handed a master key to all the locked doors; he had faced but never managed to open. "Educators who contemplate the essence of education" – this insight became his revelation. Henceforth, every task Ahmed approached was infused with this dedicated contemplation. This paradigm shifts not only enhanced his work but also sparked his imagination to challenge conventions and innovate. His expertise expanded beyond the confines of engineering, embracing literature, moving from empirical data demonstrations to the art of storytelling.

Ahmed now perpetually sought to unearth mysteries of previously unexplored realms. His greatest delight stemmed from acquiring new knowledge and putting it into practice, steadfast in his resolve never to become a mere servant to a skill, a field, or a prescribed practice.

"To think about what I am doing, not merely to do it — even if done with excellence," became Ahmed's guiding principle. This lesson radically altered the trajectory of his life.

A simple narrative, whether encountered in a book, depicted through a film's character, or uttered by a respected figure, can profoundly affect us. It can alter our perspectives, deepen our self-understanding, inspire dreams, facilitate a lateral step, help overcome fears, encourage thinking outside the conventional, resist the mundane, and indeed, it can utterly transform our life. A world devoid of stories would be a sterile one, lacking joy, passion, or ideals — a realm of automatons.

Stories touch our souls; they do not leave us unchanged. Transforming a life ranks among the most significant choices made by humans. A narrative can guide us in making such a choice.

If a story can be pivotal in deciding to change a life, it can equally influence lesser decisions in project, program, or general management. Before any decision, there must be commitment. A story aids us in committing and engaging others in our visions.

INTRODUCTION

If our era struggles to find meaning, it may be because it has forgotten how to tell stories. So perhaps, to rebuild lasting values, we must begin again — weaving narratives that uplift without overwhelming, that awaken without preaching. Simple stories... yet powerful ones. Because a people who stop telling stories also stop hoping.

There's something stirring in the air — a memory reawakening. Quietly, without fanfare, storytelling is making its return. Not as mere entertainment, but as a tool, a lever, an art of governing the invisible. Story — not the kind we date in history books, but the kind we tell — is reclaiming its place. In leadership circles, in the heart of transformation, in stakeholder engagement, in marketing, in education... It is no longer a soulful extra. It has become the language of strategy.

And that says a lot about our time. We've come to realize — or perhaps to remember — that where numbers fall short, stories resonate. Where plans collapse, stories rally. That's why storytelling skills are growing in importance today. They are becoming more refined, more precise, even taught in the most prestigious schools.

Over more than thirty years navigating the winding paths of project management, one truth — gentle yet persistent — kept returning to me: the most meaningful successes didn't come from tools or procedures. They were rooted elsewhere. In people. In relationships. And when those relationships became right — sincere, almost sacred — they always rested on one thing: trust. Not the kind you declare, but the kind you build. Slowly. Patiently. Like a bridge between two souls. It grows in the quiet of shared days, in the silent harmony of collective effort.

At the heart of that trust were precious moments. Moments of resonance. Of mutual influence. Glances exchanged in the midst of doubt, experiences lived side by side... and above all, stories. Stories we sometimes whispered without even realizing it. And with time, I came to understand — those stories were the true keys to connection.

So we began to search for them, the way you search for gold — in memories, in silences, in forgotten gestures. And we waited. For the right moment. The right heart to reach. The right vulnerability to reveal. Because yes, storytelling alone was not enough. You had to feel it. You had to earn it. And through that subtle quest, a form of perfection began to emerge — not rigid, but alive. A perfection that still evolves. That sharpens with every encounter.

It's through the human, in their rawest truth, that I've known my greatest successes. And it's through story — humble, vibrant, shared — that those successes found their breath.

The approach behind this book wasn't conceived as a showcase of fixed theories. It was born from a deeper, more tangible need: to be useful. To offer not ideas floating in the abstract, but markers. Tools. Walkable paths. In short: how to ....

Because in a world overflowing with speeches, what makes the difference is no longer what we say — but what we spark. And the act of storytelling, when done right, becomes a lever. A breath. A practical art.

Three pillars form the foundation of this approach — like an architecture both flexible and solid, a bridge cast between intention and action.

First pillar: How do we craft a story that truly moves people? Not just a sequence of events, but a narrative that pulses, that resonates. The goal is to shape a story that speaks as much to the soul as to the mind. A story that doesn't just explain, but makes you feel. That doesn't prove, but awakens. This means seeking not the spectacular, but the sincere. The genuine. The profound. Because it's not complexity that gives a story impact — it's authenticity.

Second pillar: How do we refine it, grow it, polish it without distorting it? A story, like a diamond, is never perfect on the first cut. It needs perspective, feedback, rewrites. It unfolds through trial and refinement. And it's in that process of adjustment that meaning takes shape. You learn to trim what weighs it down. To amplify what moves. To listen to the silences, it evokes. Improvement here isn't just technical editing — it's a sensitive transformation.

Third pillar: How do we adapt it to different contexts without losing its soul? A great story isn't static. It travels. It changes attire depending on the culture, the audience, the moment. But its heart always beats with the same rhythm. Adaptation isn't betrayal — it's what allows the story to live elsewhere. To reach other sensibilities. To engage with other truths.

This book, then, won't tell you what to think. Instead, it offers a stance. A lens. A way of making story not just a tool, but a companion — a force for transformation, and sometimes… a guide toward destiny.

The first part of this book is anchored in the invisible power of stories — and their ability to bring people together. Before we build, we must feel. Feel what connects. What moves. What unites. This first part lays the foundation: it explores the force of narratives across various spheres — political, organizational, and social — and reveals how a well-placed story can shift even the strongest convictions. It guides you to recognize your audience, to listen before you speak, and to carve out the core of your message — that central idea that pulses beneath the words. What follows is an alchemy workshop. This is where everything comes alive: how to give shape to a story that truly roots engagement. Not just a speech, but a breath that resonates with each stakeholder — adapting without betraying itself, speaking to the "I" while invoking the "we." A story that, through its sincerity and structure, becomes a turning point — a catalyst for collective action.

The second part of this book is rooted in the concrete. Because knowing the power of storytelling is one thing — knowing where, when, and how to breathe it into real-life situations is another. To avoid leaving the reader in abstraction, I chose a familiar compass: the PMI's project management process groups. A guiding thread. A map. From initiation to closure — through planning, execution, and monitoring — each phase becomes a potential stage for storytelling. Because yes, at every turn of the project, a narrative can emerge: to clarify a vision, rally people around a plan, overcome resistance, celebrate victories, or transform failures into shared learning. Here, storytelling is no longer a bonus. It becomes a lever. A bridge. A parallel language that flows through the entire structure of the project — giving it substance, momentum, and memory.

The third part gets to the heart of the matter. Here, it's no longer just about telling stories — it's about fine-tuning them. About aiming true. Because not all stakeholders are the same. Each has their own language, fears, triggers, and silences. This section delves into the art of adapting a narrative — not by diluting it, but by tuning it, like an instrument, to the resonance of the person or group you want to engage. Each profile, each stance, calls for a distinct narrative strategy. But before you can rally, you must recognize. Before you can mobilize, you must understand. This is where storytelling reveals another face: that of a tool for insight. A mirror held up to others — and to ourselves. The section closes with this idea: that stories can become keys to truly seeing stakeholders — not as we wish they were, but as they really are. And from that place of clarity, we can begin to weave meaning together, in a world that never stops shifting.

What matters here is not passive reading. It's not about absorbing ready-made truths carved in stone. No. What matters is the living interaction — that subtle breath between these lines and you. Between these words and your world.

This book is not an end. It's a starting point. A raw material. A fertile ground. It's up to you to draw from it what resonates. What speaks to you. What unsettles you — and that's a good thing. It's yours to turn into a foundation, a springboard, a flexible base for your own stories.

Because the most beautiful text only has value if it comes alive. If it pushes you to create. To adapt. To rewrite. To tell — not what you've read, but what you've understood, what you've felt. The goal isn't to imitate, but to ignite. To give shape to your stories — the ones that carry your voice, your struggles, yourmomentum. This book is not an answer. It's an invitation. A hand extended. A spark.

PART I: STORY POWER & TAKEHOLDERS ENGAGEMENT

I.   Story power

Let me tell you that a simple story, small it may seem, has the power to transform our perception, enrich our self-awareness, ignite our dreams, and prompt us to deviate from our usual path. It can lead us to overcome our fears, to think beyond the comforting railings of our daily lives, to challenge mundanity, and perhaps even radically change our lives. For Ahmed, it was a revelation: "To think about what I am doing and not just perform tasks, even excellently." For the person you wish to positively influence, the story could hold an even more personal and specific significance. It becomes more powerful if it connects with a crucial, often unseen aspect of their life. Let us never forget that truly understanding someone, grasping the essence of their motivations, is not only possible but absolutely essential.

" As such stories are dangerous... It is also essential to be cautious about sharing them, whether through narratives or depicted representations...," a well-known quote from

Plato in his well-known book The republic[1]. He already saw narrative as an elusive force, both divine and dangerous. He describes how myths and stories seep into the soul, shaping the morals and ethos of an entire city. According to him, truth and falsehood dance perilously close, inseparable. He also recognized the power of these narratives to instill courage, temperance, and justice. Throughout the history of humanity, myths have shaped the lives of societies and continue to do so.

As civilizations blossomed, storytelling evolved into a more sophisticated art form, embraced by Greek bards and Egyptian scribes alike. It became the scaffold upon which societies built their identities, and through which they questioned the gods and the cosmos. The epics of Homer and the scriptures of monotheistic traditions alike did not merely narrate events; they offered a lens through which to view the world, a framework by which to judge right from wrong.

In the tapestried halls of the Middle Ages, stories were the currency of human emotion, rich with the lore of knights and their noble quests. These narratives, passed from generation to generation through spoken word and then through printed page, wove the social fabric tighter, drawing communities into a shared sense of purpose and identity.

Today, in the digital epoch, the essence of storytelling remains steadfast, even as its mediums evolve. Stories now travel at the speed of light across the globe, through wires and waves, reaching millions at the click of a button. Yet, regardless of how they are transmitted, they retain their core function: to connect us, to make us feel less alone, to help us navigate the complexities of human existence.

Fig 1: Story power

Storytelling transcends mere entertainment; it taps into a profound, scientifically substantiated mechanism that drives human change. Our neural pathways are intricately fashioned to resonate with narratives—a discovery not merely anecdotal but backed by robust scientific inquiry. Recent studies illuminate how immersing oneself in fiction amplifies empathy[2]. This is no small feat: psychologists and neuroscientists have demonstrated that narratives activate brain regions essential for understanding the emotions and thoughts of others. Through the lens of functional magnetic resonance imaging, we see how narratives sculpt our behaviors—metaphors and vivid descriptions ignite our sensory cortex, sparking regions associated with insight, action, and movement.[3]

Our visceral response to stories is also underpinned by a chemical dance. Dopamine, released during emotionally charged moments, enhances our recollection of these events, embedding them deeply in our memory. Thus, if the goal is memorability, a compelling story invariably triumphs over dry statistics. Furthermore, oxytocin, released during character-driven narratives, fosters a spirit of cooperation among listeners. To rally support for a cause, craft your stories with a personal, human touch.[4]

These physiological reactions to storytelling reveal why narratives resonate so profoundly. They stick with us, echoing long after the closing credits of a powerful film or the final page of a gripping novel.

In the realm of business, where analytics often reign supreme, storytelling remains a critical tool for inspiring innovation. Despite the day's demands — donning power suits, organizing briefcases — we remain innately human, moved by stories that touch our hearts and minds, altering us and those we share them with.

The power of narrative is especially pivotal when we venture into the uncharted waters of future possibilities. The potential of a novel idea cannot be validated analytically in advance; it lacks historical data to forecast its interaction with the world. The art of storytelling prevails — transforming complex, abstract ideas into relatable, emotionally charged narratives that resonate with audiences, seeing themselves reflected in the tale.

Great leaders harness this narrative power to envision and articulate what might be, before making it a reality. A compelling story can persuade people to venture beyond the familiar, embracing new ideas with enthusiasm. Recall a moment when a story captivated you completely, erasing the boundaries of the room, focusing your entire being on the narrative unfurling before you. This is the power of storytelling at its most profound.

Recent work in cognitive neuroscience[5] informs us that humans do not make decisions rationally and logically only; the truth is that they also decide emotionally and subconsciously, sometimes irrationally, and justify these decisions rationally. In every major decision, there is a story at play, a narrative pattern that guides action. When a leader decides to embark on a new entrepreneurial venture, they do not rely solely on market studies and financial projections; they envision a future, a vision in which this decision leads them somewhere. When Steve Jobs returned to Apple in 1997, he imposed a new story on the company: one of creative renewal, of a product that would be more than just a tool, but a companion for every individual. He told this vision so powerfully that it guided every strategic choice, transforming Apple into an innovation giant. Every leader, whether a parent guiding their family or a head of state charting the destiny of a people, constructs their narrative, imbued with their values, their dreams, and also their fears. This narrative, often, is more decisive than the facts themselves.

Emotions make narratives alive; they allow everyone to project themselves, to feel intensely and identify with the main characters. When a doctor tells a family how he struggled to save a life, he does not deliver a mere medical report; he shares a story of struggle, hope, and dedication, and it is this story that creates an unbreakable bond. In our personal relationships, as in the narratives of the media, through the emotions they convey, emotion is what seals memory, what transforms information into shared experience. A well-told story is a powerful vehicle for emotions.

Children remember the stories of their childhood long after they have forgotten the rules of grammar! Narratives are mnemonic capsules, structured patterns that transform raw information into unforgettable mental images. Consider the case of memorization techniques. By linking each fact to an image, a story, it is easily remembered. This is how generations have retained the Bible, the Quran, the foundational stories of world cultures. The structure of a narrative acts like a compass in our mind, allowing us to navigate the complexity of knowledge, to connect disparate elements. In our lives, we meet many people, we forget them days after, except those who have impacted us with their stories. However, if we encounter a character in a novel that we liked, they will stay with us during our life. Modern businesses use this principle: to teach values, they tell founding stories, anecdotes that resonate with employees, much more than a simple charter of rules.

Narratives can unite or destroy, elevate or degrade. Stories have a singular power: they capture the imagination, transform perception, and most importantly, they act as gateways into ideological worlds where judgment is suspended. Extremists have long understood that, to transform a man into a soldier of a cause, it is not enough to talk to him – he must be immersed, made to live an epic where every word becomes a step towards an absolute truth. Extremism knows how to feed on simplified stories, binary narratives where the world is divided into "us against them." The hero is pure, ready to sacrifice his life for an ideal, while the enemy is corrupt, a symbol of a pervasive and omnipresent threat. By simplifying the world into a Manichean confrontation of light and darkness, these narratives appeal to the heart more than the mind. They relieve doubt, end complexity, and offer individuals a simplified moral map, where every action seems justified, where violence becomes a defensive necessity. At the heart of this narrative strategy, there is a mechanism of identification. Extremist narratives do not merely describe ideas; they invite individuals to become actors, heroes of their own story. Thus, the power of stories in extremism lies in this ability to encapsulate worldviews where complexity is banned, were empathy fades behind rigid certainties. These narratives do not simply build an ideology; they build a mental space where emotions dominate reason, and where adherence to a cause becomes an undeniable truth. Under this narrative grip, the individual is lost to become part of a whole, blinded by the deceptive beauty of a story that promises an ideal in exchange for the abandonment of his humanity.

Politics is the art of telling a collective narrative, of steering the nation towards an ideal. In the United States, the American dream, this promise of "social ascent for those who work hard," is a narrative that has shaped the country's identity. John F. Kennedy, by promising to put a man on the moon, created a collective challenge that transcended political differences. In each country, the political narrative is a tool for building an identity and directing the people. In this sense, political speeches are often not mere words: they are narratives that can build or deconstruct entire societies. The power of narratives in contexts of political conflicts is fascinating, somewhat like the score of a symphony that seeks to dominate the emotions of each listener. This art of manipulating narratives becomes a subtle science, a game of symbols and words that transcends facts to anchor themselves in collective imaginations, where each phrase becomes a brushstroke in the complex canvas of human emotions. Political narratives act like modern legends. They magnify, sometimes to the point of distortion, ideals, values, and even sufferings to weave heroes and antagonists. Beyond the visible conflict, there exists an invisible war, that of the imagination, where each party attempts to anchor its discourse in the mind of its people, as an absolute truth, a beacon that illuminates the way. The effectiveness of a narrative in politics lies in its ability to evoke identification: it tells the wounds, hopes, frustrations, and resilience of those who listen, offering them a place within a narrative that transcends their individual lives.

Great leaders are not just strategists; they are storytellers. Winston Churchill, during World War II, was able to galvanize an entire nation with his fiery speeches, drawing a narrative of resilience, courage, and victory. He made each Briton an actor in this national epic, transforming despair into hope. From Mandela to Martin Luther King, great leaders know that their words are seeds of conviction, sparks of inspiration. They provide direction, meaning, a reason to fight for something greater than oneself. They had the power to tell stories.

When introducing change in an organization, resistance arises. It is the narrative that comes to soothe these fears, transforming uncertainty into opportunity. By creating a narrative around learning and curiosity, then leader could breathe new energy. Collaborators, instead of seeing change as a threat, perceived it as a collective journey, a shared challenge. The power of narration in management is what allows transforming each collaborator into an actor of change. Effective selling is not just a material exchange; it is a promise of emotions, of experiences. A good salesman of a product, service, idea, vision, or change, does not describe what he wants to sell; he tells what he can transform in the life of the buyer. The power of narration in sales is to offer a story, to make each purchase meaningful, to weave an emotional link between the object and the buyer.

In the solitude of thoughts, a story can metamorphose into an emotional compass, a silent guide that orients, reorients, and ultimately redefines the individual from within. It is there, in this intimate depth, that the battles of the soul are played out. The narrative becomes a mirror, an echo, and almost the very fabric of thought. Each individual carries within them a dominant narrative, this story that colors their perceptions and subtly modifies their reactions. When a narrative is invited into our mind, it does not just tell itself; it shapes the very way we understand the world. And when a story finds fertile ground, it takes root, enchants, reinvents itself with each internal questioning. It becomes that mute friend, that companion who whispers subjective truths, but unshakeable. The power of intra-individual narratives lies in their ability to become prisms through which everything is observed, judged, experienced. They transform perceptions into convictions. Thus, a simple memory, a heard phrase, a exchanged look, can take on an enormous magnitude, enrich in a meaning that exceeds the moment. The story, once anchored, weaves a subtle web in the mind of the individual, a web where each thread is a belief, a feeling, a certainty. Thus, stories have this power to manage oneself and manage others. In these times where uncertainty is certain and waves of complexity arrive from everywhere, the power to structure disparate and incomplete information has become a necessary skill for any leader wanting to lead any project of change to success.

Throughout the ages, the story of humanity has been built on ideas. The intellectual, whether a scientist or philosopher, has delved into the depths of their intellect to craft visions, theories, and truths. But an idea, no matter how brilliant, only lives if it is transmitted. This is where the storyteller steps in, the bearer of tales, adept at wrapping meaning in narratives that touch the heart as much as the mind. It matters not whether the idea is benign or malign; it takes root and flourishes in their hands.

The storyteller, wields narrative as an artist sculpts raw stone. His ambition? To inspire, to move, to etch ideas into memories. His audience is universal: from children who dream to sages who reflect, spanning all cultures and horizons. But what gives him strength is his approach: characters grounded in tangible conflicts; plots woven with emotions that resonate with the rhythm of human experiences. An idea, through his words, ceases to be an abstraction. It becomes alive, embodied, unforgettable. However, behind this narrative magic lies a paradox. While the storyteller touches hearts, he can also manipulate them. By simplifying, by amplifying, he sometimes bends the truth for emotional impact. Indeed, what he conveys embeds itself in minds not because it is accurate, but because it is felt.

Nothing imprints on the soul more deeply than a story charged with emotions. Think of your life: how many faces you've met have faded over time? But a character from a beloved novel remains. He becomes a part of you, a silent companion. Stories transform information into experience. They do not merely speak to us; they inhabit us.

In the hushed, infinite corridors of time, storytelling emerges not merely as an activity but as the very lifeblood of human connection. Each narrative, spun from the threads of yore, carries the breath of its teller and the whispers of ages past. These tales, scrawled on cave walls with ochre or shared beside flickering fires, were not crafted for mere amusement but as the sinews binding human experience across the chasms of time and space.

49

II.   How to target stakeholders

Story: Put himself in the other's Shoes

Our friend Hamid, once a project director at the heart of a vibrant research and development department, ardently believed in the power of the new solutions he crafted. He envisioned these creations in the hands of a promotional entity, tasked with forging commercial and partnership ties to spark potential clients' interest. However, in an ironic twist of fate, this very entity seemed to hinder more than facilitate the journey of these innovations, sometimes even trampling the opportunity to capitalize on these technological gems. It upsets him

One day, weary and as if a distrust had taken hold of him regarding the commercial department's abilities, Hamid decided to bypass the established process. He set out to find an ally on his own to develop a solution with strong commercial potential together. This bold move was not without consequences, as it met with scathing criticism from the concerned department, armed with evidence that the new partner lacked financial stability, based on in-depth analyses of its stock market performance.

The conflict soon escalated, turning every interaction into a battlefield where each department entrenched itself, thereby increasing mutual reluctance and mistrust. Decisions, usually swift, were now delayed, stretching out timelines sometimes beyond reason. Meetings, far from reconciling viewpoints, ended in deadlocks, with misunderstandings piling up like dead leaves in autumn.

Faced with this toxic impasse, the executive leadership decided it was time to restructure. In this shake-up, Hamid was appointed to take the helm of the commercial department. Carried by a whirlwind of ideas to inject new dynamism, he was stunned to discover that numerous files were stagnating, hindered by partners reluctant to honor their initial commitments.

After much reflection and numerous workshops, he formed a conviction: henceforth, each partner would have to meet minimum criteria to forge lasting relationships. To his own surprise, and that of everyone else, he became more stringent than his predecessors. Recalling his past frictions, he wished he had had the opportunity earlier to lead this entity, to put himself in the shoes of those he had once criticized.

From then on, with every new challenge, he made an effort to put himself in the other's shoes, to understand their needs, to see through their eyes, and to feel with their heart. He never passed up an opportunity to briefly stand in someone else's place. This allowed him to gain perspective, efficiency, resources, healthy human relations, and productivity. What would you do in the same context?

Background to target stakeholders

In the previous narrative, faced with each obstacle, Hamid fully immersed himself in the experiences of others. He strove to understand their needs, to embrace their worldviews, and to feel the reality with their senses. He seized every opportunity to momentarily step into another's life. This practice granted him a wealth of perspectives, boosted his efficiency, enriched his resources, strengthened his human relationships, and greatly increased his productivity. However, it was not about losing his identity in that of another. Rather, it was about positioning himself to defend the interests of the initiative, and much more! It is crucial to have the wisdom to see how to harmoniously merge the aspirations of the stakeholders with those of the project. This process is only feasible by adopting a new perspective and blending the two viewpoints. This is what is referred to as taking a meta-position.[1]

Stakeholder is person who could be affected positively or negatively by the process or the result of the initiative be it program or project[2]. However, as Robert McKee said[3]: People experience far more that they express. Effort is needed to characterize the stakeholder in order to discover his deep need. One might discover that the first perceptual position is not merely a viewpoint but a profound engagement with the self. This position, which we call the "Self" stance, invites one to delve deeply into the intricacies of their own psyche, examining every thought, emotion, and sensory touch that paints their personal reality. This journey into the self is not just reflective; it is revelatory, unraveling the layers of personal consciousness and highlighting how external realities influence our inner dialogues. It is essential, then, for cultivating a rich understanding of oneself, revealing the core of our thoughts and emotions in relation to the world around us.

Fig 2: Target stakeholders

Venturing into the second perceptual position, often known as the "Other," one embarks on an empathetic odyssey into another's soul. Here, you transcend your own confines and imaginatively inhabit the life and perspective of another. This act of stepping into another's shoes is not a mere exercise of imagination but a profound gesture of understanding and connection. It is through this perspective that one can truly comprehend the motivations and emotions that drive others, thereby enriching our interactions and fostering deeper human connections. In both personal and professional realms, this understanding can be transformative, unraveling the complex web of human relations.

The third stance, the "Observer" or "Meta" position, calls for a panoramic view of the tableau of interaction. From this elevated perch, one observes the interplay between self and others with the detachment of a sage observer. This perspective is not about disengagement but about achieving a higher clarity that comes from distance. It allows one to discern patterns, dynamics, and underlying implications that remain obscured within the fray of emotional engagement. This strategic vantage point is instrumental in resolving conflicts and cultivating a nuanced understanding of complex situations, thereby guiding one towards more enlightened decisions and interactions.

How to target stakeholders

We need to characterize stakeholders. We need to identify all observable traits and outer behaviors but we all know that all those information are largely the masks or personae that a stakeholder wears as he carries out his relationship with others. We need to listen with our eyes and watch with our ears. The goal is to discover what stakeholders really value and care about. We need to take a stakeholder as system pay attention to what he says, do, think and fell.

The triggers of behavior are foundational in understanding what drives stakeholder actions and decisions. These prompts can be environmental cues, emotional states, or specific circumstances that lead to particular responses. By identifying these triggers, one can anticipate reactions and tailor approaches that align with stakeholder expectations and needs. It's akin to understanding the wind that propels a ship — knowing the direction and strength can guide the journey more effectively.

The values and concerns of stakeholders often dictate their priorities and decisions. Paying attention to what stakeholders care deeply about, such as safety, efficiency, or integrity, can provide insights into their decision-making processes and what they are most likely to support. This understanding allows for crafting messages and solutions that resonate on a personal level, thus fostering trust and engagement.

Non-verbal cues often communicate more than words can convey. Observing body language helps in understanding the unspoken feelings and reactions of stakeholders, providing a deeper insight into their true sentiments regarding a project or proposal. This level of understanding is crucial for adjusting strategies and interactions to more effectively align with stakeholder emotions and reactions.

Adopting a systemic view looking deep to patterns in behavior or feedback can signal underlying trends or issues that might not be immediately apparent. Recognizing these patterns can lead to predictions of future behaviors or reveal systemic issues that need addressing. Just like a weaver spots flaws and strengths in the fabric pattern, identifying these behavioral patterns can help in strengthening stakeholder relationships and refining project approaches.

Adjustments that stakeholders make in response to their environment or challenges they face. are invaluable in understanding how they cope with change and what solutions they devise to meet their needs. From There one can design interventions that are more aligned with the natural adjustments stakeholders are inclined to make, ensuring smoother implementation and higher acceptance.

Using open-ended questions in stakeholder interviews is crucial as it allows for a free-flowing, comprehensive exchange of information. That encourages stakeholders to express their thoughts, experiences, and emotions in detail, rather than restricting them to yes or no responses. This approach enables the interviewer to gain a deeper understanding of the stakeholder's needs, expectations, and any underlying issues that might not surface through closed questioning.

Asking 'why' multiple times during interviews is an effective method for digging deeper into each response a stakeholder provides, mirroring an investigative approach that seeks to uncover the root cause of perceptions, decisions, or issues. It helps in peeling back the layers of surface-level information, akin to peeling an onion, to reveal core insights about stakeholder needs and challenges. It is reminiscent of the Five Whys technique in problem-solving, which is aimed at exploring the cause-and-effect relationships underlying a particular problem. As noted by Ohno[4] the originator of this technique within the Toyota Production System, this method is instrumental in understanding the essence of problems and can be just as powerful in comprehending stakeholder motivations and deeper needs.

Engaging with stakeholders involves consciously setting aside one's preconceived notions and opinions to truly listen and understand the stakeholder's point of view. By doing so we ensure that the data collected is not tainted by their own beliefs or the interviewer's agenda, thus maintaining the integrity and validity of the information. This practice is crucial for achieving genuine empathy and objectivity, which are pivotal in accurately capturing stakeholder needs and experiences. Kvale and Brinkmann[5] stress the importance of the interviewer's neutrality, suggesting that a non-judgmental, open stance during interviews fosters a more truthful and profound communication. Limiting oneself in this way is a discipline that enhances the quality and reliability of qualitative research findings.

When it is possible, do it yourself in order to go beyond intellectual understanding and obtain a more visceral sense of another's perspective. Empathy experiences are important because they help us to put ourselves in the shoes of the people we're designing for. Sharing these emotional experiences helps bond and align colleagues and clients around a common goal. This empathetic approach allows us to grasp not just the surface requirements but the deeper motivations and challenges that shape their expectations and needs. It requires a genuine connection and a willingness to experience the world from the stakeholder's viewpoint. This is not merely a process but a journey into the heart of another's world, where every detail can reveal profound truths about their desires and pain points. It mirrors the method actors employ, living their roles to fully embody the characters they portray. By doing so, we uncover nuances that typical analytical approaches might overlook, leading to more effective and tailored solutions that resonate on a deeper level with the stakeholders involved. This method is not just effective but necessary, as supported by insights from fields such as design thinking and user experience research, which emphasize the value of deep empathy to foster innovation and responsiveness (Tim Brown "Change by Design", IDEO, 2009)[6].

How to adapt and create your own story

	Chapter story	Your own story
The challenge	Hamid ardently believed in the power of the new solutions he crafted. However, in an ironic twist of fate, this very entity seemed to hinder more than facilitate the journey of these innovations	
Descending crisis	Hamid decided to bypass the established process. This bold move was not without consequences, as it met with scathing criticism from the concerned department,	
Rock Bottom	Decisions, usually swift, were now delayed, stretching out timelines sometimes beyond reason.	
The worst/rebirth	Faced with this toxic impasse, the executive leadership decided it was time to restructure. In this shake-up, Hamid was appointed to take the helm of the commercial department.	
The discovery	stunned to discover that numerous files were stagnating, hindered by	

	Chapter story	Your own story
	partners reluctant to honor their initial commitments.	
The rise	each partner would have to meet minimum criteria to forge lasting relationships.	
The return	To his own surprise, and that of everyone else, he became more stringent than his predecessors.	
The lesson	From then on, with every new challenge, he made an effort to put himself in the other's shoes, to understand their needs, to see through their eyes, and to feel with their heart.	
Call to action	What would you do in the same context?	

Takeaways

- We need to characterize stakeholders (first perceptual position).

- The empathetic approach (second perceptual position) allows us to grasp not just the surface requirements but the deeper motivations and challenges that shape their expectations and needs.

- Use the third perceptual position in order to synthetize all the information gathered and better target the stakeholders.

- The values and concerns of stakeholders often dictate their priorities and decisions.

- Non-verbal cues often communicate more than words can convey.

- Patterns in behavior or feedback can signal underlying trends or issues that might not be immediately apparent.

- After Open-question, asking 'why' multiple times during interviews is an effective method for digging deeper into each response a stakeholder provides.

- It is essential to limit one's assumptions and biases during the interview process.

How to improve

	Chapter story	Your own story
Make it personal	Our friend Hamid,	
Get emotional	It upsets him… One day, weary and as if a distrust had taken hold of him regarding the commercial department's abilities… To his own surprise, and that of everyone else, he became more stringent than his predecessors.	
Use anecdote, metaphor or reflection	Meetings, far from reconciling viewpoints, ended in deadlocks, with misunderstandings piling up like dead leaves in autumn.	
Make it visual: Sensory channel of the audience in order to build report	The conflict soon escalated, turning every interaction into a battlefield where each department entrenched itself, thereby increasing mutual reluctance and mistrust	
Give a call to action	What would you do in the same context.	
Stay inspired	One way to improve drastically this story is to let the stakeholder to tell his own story	

III.   How to build the master idea to tell

Story: She learned to better articulate her needs

Karima, a young engineer passionate about natural resources, never stopped honing her expertise. After earning her PhD, she continued her research independently and taught as an adjunct at the university. Despite her proven skills, opportunities to fully utilize them within her company were rare. Gradually, she considered dedicating herself entirely to teaching, reducing her professional engagement, which led to tensions with her supervisor.

One day, an unexpected proposal from the HR department emerged: to lead a division following an imminent departure. For Karima, this additional responsibility seemed to conflict with her academic aspirations. Therefore, she firmly declined the offer.

Internal conflicts intensified, fueled by her boss's criticisms suggesting she was shirking her responsibilities. Each meeting, every new proposal, seemed only to escalate the conflict. Working under these conditions became increasingly oppressive each day.

The situation reached a climax when an ultimatum was issued: accept the proposal or resign. In her search for advice, Karima turned to a long-standing *colleague known for his wisdom and experience. To her great surprise, he revealed the hidden opportunities of the position: enriching encounters and the chance to actively participate in the company's research and development efforts, which promised to be even more rewarding.*

This revelation was a true epiphany for her.

- *"Why didn't the HR manager present it to me this way?" she wondered. "It was exactly what I was looking for."*
- *"He should have recognized your true need: to engage in research that is both valued and valuable," her colleague explained. "Knowing how to express your needs is crucial, but a good manager must also be able to put themselves in others' shoes to truly understand their expectations. Otherwise, he will continually be managing artificial conflicts."*

Since this realization, Karima agreed to lead the proposed division. She learned to better articulate her needs and empathetically put herself in the shoes of her counterparts. This new approach radically transformed how she managed her professional relationships and, by extension, her entire career.

Karima herself was transformed, realizing the importance of deeply linking her aspirations to the opportunities presented to her. What's about you?

Background to build the story idea

In the previous story, we realized the importance of deeply understanding a stakeholder's needs.

This revelation was a true epiphany for Karima as it is revealed in this dialogue.

- Why didn't the HR manager present it to me this way? she wondered. "It was exactly what I was looking for."

- He should have recognized your true need: to engage in research that is both valued and valuable, her colleague explained. Knowing how to express your needs is crucial, but a good manager must also be able to put themselves in others' shoes to truly understand their expectations. Otherwise, they will constantly be managing artificial conflicts."

Now, beyond that, imagine that you have created a story where the main idea revolves around the deep needs of the stakeholder. You won't just engage them by satisfying their needs but also, you will truly change their life. They will remember you for a lifetime! Below is how.

"We begin with the premise, which is your entire story condensed to a single sentence. That premise will suggest the essence of the story, and we will use that to figure out how to develop it so as to get the most out of the idea." [1]

Fig3: Master idea to tell

When synthesizing the deep needs of a stakeholder, it's essential to distill their desires and necessities into a clear and concise message. Firstly, elucidating what stakeholders need and want requires an understanding that goes beyond the superficial; it involves peeling back layers to reveal the core motivations driving their actions and decisions. This clarity not only guides project objectives but also aligns team efforts towards fulfilling these fundamental desires.

At this step the deep need should be understood and formulated in concise and memorable way be it relating to an opportunity or a problem. When addressing the deep-seated needs of a stakeholder, the formulation of a proposal must not only resonate with their immediate demands but also align strategically with their broader goals and aspirations. This approach transcends the superficial layer of requirement gathering to delve into a profound understanding of the stakeholder's context, pressures, and future vision. In crafting such a proposal, it is essential to weave a narrative that encapsulates not only what is needed but why it is vital, blending empathy with practicality.

The language used to convey these needs must resonate on an emotional level. Language is not merely a tool for communication but a vehicle for inspiration. By choosing words that evoke emotions, one can galvanize a team into action, transforming passive participants into active contributors. The narrative should stir something within the audience, compelling them to engage deeply and personally with the project's goals.

The articulation of these needs should be memorable and shareable. It must stick in the mind, becoming a mantra that can easily be passed along within the team and beyond. This aspect of communication is crucial for fostering a communal understanding and commitment to the stakeholder's vision.

How to build the story idea

A compelling big idea for a short story should pivot around a central problem or conflict that not only drives the narrative but also captivates the audience interest. When crafting this idea, think about a challenge or dilemma that your characters must confront, which in turn reflects a larger, relatable issue faced by your audience. This problem should be deep enough to explore through various facets and consequences, enabling the story to unfold in a manner that offers both tension and intrigue. Consider problems that you are passionate about or that resonate deeply with you, as this personal connection can often translate into a more engaging and authentic narrative. The problem should be specific enough to provide clear direction for the story but universal enough to resonate with a diverse audience. This balancing act between specificity and relatability is crucial in crafting a story that feels both unique and meaningful.

As Robert Mackee said:" A controlling idea may be expressed is a single sentence describing how and why life undergoes change from one condition of existence at the beginning to another at the end"[2]

A big idea is compelling if it hooks the reader immediately and sustains interest throughout the story. This involves a blend of originality and emotional engagement. The idea should offer a new perspective or a fresh take on familiar themes, challenging the reader's expectations or presenting characters with choices that provoke empathy or debate. To test the compelling nature of your idea, consider whether it raises questions that demand answers, or if it involves stakes high enough to make the reader care about the outcomes. The compelling nature often lies in the dynamics between characters, the intensity of their desires, or the critical nature of their circumstances. A truly compelling idea not only holds the reader's attention but also leaves them thinking about the implications after the story ends.

Clarity and conciseness in your big idea are paramount for ensuring that the essence of your story is immediately understandable and memorable. This means distilling your concept to its most basic elements without oversimplifying the complexities that make the story rich and engaging. A clear and concise idea should succinctly communicate who the main characters are, what they want or need, what stands in their way, and what's at stake if they fail or succeed. This clarity helps during the writing process to maintain focus and ensure every scene and character action is aligned with moving the story forward. For the audience, it means being able to grasp the narrative's direction and purpose from the outset, enhancing their engagement and satisfaction with the story.

Crafting the big idea of a short story into a single, rhyming sentence is a creative endeavor that marries brevity with the beauty of verse. This technique not only captures the essence of the narrative in a memorable and engaging way but also challenges the writer to distill complex themes and plots into their purest form. A rhyme lends a rhythmic quality to the idea, making it more appealing and easier to recall, which can intrigue readers and set a lyrical tone for the story itself.

To write a big idea in a rhyming sentence, start by identifying the central theme or conflict of your story. Focus on what is unique about your narrative—whether it's the characters, the setting, or the plot twist. Then, think about how you can express this element in a concise way that still evokes emotion or curiosity. Use a rhyming dictionary or think of common rhyme schemes to help you find words that not only describe your story's essence but also sing in harmony. This approach does more than summarize; it enchants, ensuring that the heart of your story resonates even before the first page is turned.

How to adapt and create your own story

	Chapter story	Your own story
The challenge	After earning her PhD, she continued her research independently and taught as an adjunct at the university. Despite her proven skills, opportunities to fully utilize them within her company were rare	
Descending crisis	Internal conflicts intensified, fueled by her boss's criticisms suggesting she was shirking her responsibilities. Each meeting, every new proposal, seemed only to escalate the conflict. Working under these conditions became increasingly oppressive each day.	
Rock Bottom	The situation reached a climax when an ultimatum was issued: accept the proposal or resign	

	Chapter story	**Your own story**
The worst/re birth	To her great surprise, he revealed the hidden opportunities of the position: enriching encounters and the chance to actively participate in the company's research and development efforts, which promised to be even more rewarding.	
The discover y	This revelation was a true epiphany for her. "Why didn't the HR manager present it to me this way?" she wondered. "It was exactly what I was looking for."	
The rise	Since this realization, Karima agreed to lead the proposed division. She learned to better articulate her needs and empathetically put herself in the shoes of her counterparts.	

	Chapter story	**Your own story**
The return	This new approach radically transformed how she managed her professional relationships	
The lesson	Karima herself was transformed, realizing the importance of deeply linking her aspirations to the opportunities presented to her.	
Call to action	What's about you?	

Takeaways

- A compelling big idea for a short story should pivot around a central problem or conflict that not only drives the narrative but also captivates the reader's interest.

- A big idea is compelling if it hooks the reader immediately and sustains interest throughout the story.

- Clarity and conciseness in your big idea are paramount for ensuring that the essence of your story is immediately understandable and memorable.

- Crafting the big idea of a short story into a single, rhyming sentence is a creative endeavor that marries brevity with the beauty of verse.

IV. How to construct a story to tell

Story: what I do know is that it is in your hands

Extract from: Toni Morrison Nobel Lecture December 7, 1993 [1]

"Once upon a time there was an old woman. Blind. Wise."

In the version I know the woman is the daughter of slaves, black, American, and lives alone in a small house outside of town. Her reputation for wisdom is without peer and without question. Among her people she is both the law and its transgression. The honor she is paid and the awe in which she is held reach beyond her neighborhood to places far away; to the city where the intelligence of rural prophets is the source of much amusement.

One day the woman is visited by some young people who seem to be bent on disproving her clairvoyance and showing her up for the fraud they believe she is. Their plan is simple: they enter her house and ask the one question the answer to which rides solely on her difference from them, a difference they regard as a profound disability: her blindness. They stand before her, and one of them says, "Old woman, I hold in my hand a bird. Tell me whether it is living or dead."

She does not answer, and the question is repeated. "Is the bird I am holding living or dead?"

Still she doesn't answer. She is blind and cannot see her visitors, let alone what is in their hands. She does not know their color, gender or homeland. She only knows their motive.

The old woman's silence is so long, the young people have trouble holding their laughter.

Finally she speaks and her voice is soft but stern. "I don't know", she says. "I don't know whether the bird you are holding is dead or alive, but what I do know is that it is in your hands. It is in your hands."

Her answer can be taken to mean: if it is dead, you have either found it that way or you have killed it. If it is alive, you can still kill it. Whether it is to stay alive, it is your decision. Whatever the case, it is your responsibility. »

Background of how to construct a story to tell

However brief it may be, the preceding story carries the weight of centuries. Its longevity and its journey across cultures owe nothing to its form or length, but everything to its depth. It whispers a forgotten truth: that humans are accountable not only for their actions, but also for their words. The deeper a story dives into the soul's abyss, the more likely it is to root itself in the universal. And though settings may shift, though languages may sing in different tones, the essence remains unchanged. This is the secret of myths — their grounding in what is unchanging within us.

A story rich in depth casts a wide net. A true story is a wave that transcends borders, eras, and souls. It stirs the heart and the mind alike. What follows is not a manual. It is a call. A call to craft stories that endure — because they move. Because they elevate. Because they unveil.

Storytelling, that ancient tapestry of human expression, transcends mere communication—it's an art form that bridges the divide between past and present, myth and reality. Master storytellers don't just recount events; they breathe life into them, weaving a narrative so vivid that listeners can see, hear, and feel the world they describe. This craft is not confined to the mere arrangement of words but rather in the ability to paint pictures in the mind's eye, stir the soul, and ignite imaginations.

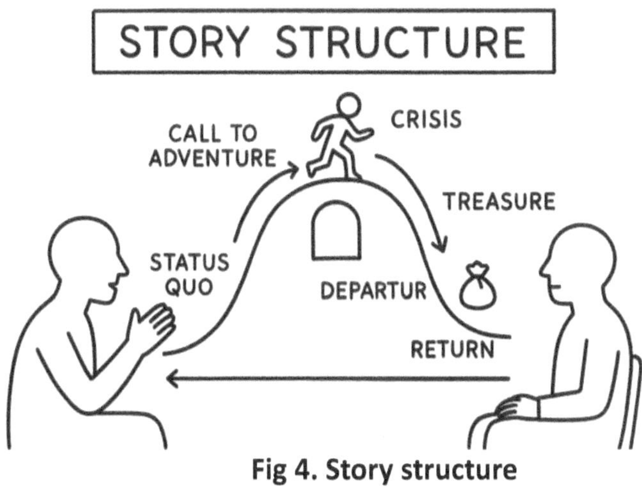

Fig 4. Story structure

At its heart, storytelling is an intimate dance between the narrative and the audience, a shared journey through landscapes both familiar and fantastical. The storyteller's voice becomes a conduit for truths wrapped in fiction, characters that feel as real as any flesh and blood person we know. Through the art of storytelling, we are transported across the boundaries of time and space, visiting ancient civilizations or futuristic worlds with equal ease. This art form is not bound by the pedestrian task of simple fact-telling. Instead, it revels in the freedom to embellish, to explore the what-ifs of history, and to delve into the human psyche. Whether through the written word, a cinematic masterpiece, or a performance that captivates the senses, storytelling adapts its shape to fit the mold of its medium, each form lending its unique flavor to the narrative essence.

Storytelling also serves as a custodian of culture, safeguarding the folklore and wisdom of generations. Each tale spun is not just a story but a legacy, encapsulating the morals, dreams, and fears of a community. This archival function of storytelling is crucial—it acts as a cultural memory bank, preserving knowledge and heritage against the erosion of time. Today, as we stand on the brink of digital frontiers, storytelling continues to evolve, embracing new technologies that enhance its reach and depth. Yet, despite these advancements, the core of storytelling remains unchanged: it is the art of making us feel deeply, think profoundly, and see the invisible. It is, in every sense, a mirror reflecting the human condition, an art form as vital as it is venerable.

The appreciation of beauty in art often elicits a profound *emotional response that can vary widely among individuals. This response is rooted in what we perceive as harmonious, balanced, or pleasing, whether in visual art, music, literature, or performance. The emotional reactions might include, Pleasure: The simple enjoyment of something that is beautiful to the viewer or listener, often leading to a sense of satisfaction or contentment; Awe: A stronger emotional response that involves a feeling of being overwhelmed by the beauty or grandeur of the artwork, which can lead to a sense of wonder or amazement and most importantly Transcendence: Experiencing a sense of beauty can elevate a person's state of being, making them feel part of something larger than themselves or connecting them to a realm of the extraordinary or sublime.

Storytelling as an Art does more than evoke raw emotions; it also engages the intellect and invites contemplation, Provocation of Thought: Art often challenges viewers to think critically about subjects, question their assumptions, and consider different perspectives, Reflection: After encountering art, individuals may reflect on the themes, techniques, or messages presented, leading to a deeper understanding or new insights about life, society, or personal experiences, Educational: Art serves as an educational tool, offering historical insights, societal critiques, or philosophical discussions that enrich the viewer's knowledge and understanding.

Storytelling's ability to forge personal connections and foster empathy is one of its most profound effects Narrative Empathy: Through narratives in literature, film, or theater, individuals can identify with characters, feel their emotions, and gain insights into their experiences, promoting a deeper sense of empathy and understanding; Shared Experience: Attending live performances or viewings can create a communal emotional experience, bonding people through shared reactions and feelings; Mirror Neurons: The concept of mirror neurons [2] suggests that observing emotions expressed in art can activate similar emotional responses in the viewer's brain, enhancing feelings of connection and understanding.

The notion of transcendence in aesthetic experiences speaks to a deeply human capacity to surpass ordinary experience and touch upon something greater, more profound, or otherwordly through encounters with beauty and art. This phenomenon is rooted in the idea that art can evoke a sense of the sublime, an aesthetic concept that has been discussed extensively in the history of philosophy and art criticism.

Complexity, the need for meaning and storytelling

In a world marked by rapid technological advances and shifting societal norms, change has become a constant. This persistent state of flux not only drives innovation but also breeds complexity, making it increasingly difficult for individuals and organizations to navigate their environments effectively. Amidst this evolving landscape, the quest for meaning emerges as a crucial anchor, providing clarity and purpose.

Change, by its very nature, disrupts the status quo, challenging existing frameworks and compelling individuals to adapt. It's not merely about technological or economic shifts; it encompasses cultural and social transformations as well. As these changes accumulate, they weave a complex tapestry of interdependencies and consequences, often unforeseen and misunderstood. This complexity can be overwhelming, as it demands continuous learning and flexibility from all stakeholders involved.

However, it's the human response to this complexity that truly defines the outcomes. When faced with change, people seek understanding and coherence; they yearn for a narrative that makes sense of the chaos. This need for meaning is deeply ingrained in the human psyche—a core aspect of our nature that helps us navigate life's uncertainties. Meaning provides a sense of continuity, offering a lens through which the past, present, and future can be integrated into a cohesive whole.

In organizational contexts, leaders play a pivotal role in crafting and disseminating this sense of meaning. They are tasked with interpreting changes and complexities in a way that aligns with the organization's values and vision. Effective leadership transforms the challenges posed by change into opportunities for growth and innovation. It involves creating a shared vision that motivates and inspires, turning potential anxieties about the unknown into collective aspirations.

Moreover, in a broader societal context, the need for meaning influences cultural narratives and public discourse. Societies that manage to embed meaningful narratives into their cultural fabric are better equipped to sustain cohesion and resilience in the face of change. These narratives can foster a sense of belonging and commitment, helping individuals feel valued and understood, which is essential for social stability and progress.

As we navigate the complexities of modern life, the interplay between change, complexity, and the need for meaning becomes increasingly significant. Whether in personal growth, organizational development, or societal evolution, understanding and addressing this dynamic is key to fostering resilience and achieving sustained success. Embracing change, managing complexity, and cultivating meaning are not just strategies but essential skills for thriving in today's world.

Kenneth Burke's concept of "equipment for living"[5] is one of his most profound contributions to literary and rhetorical theory. He argued that stories are not merely entertainment; they serve as practical tools that help individuals navigate life's complexities, make decisions, and interpret their experiences. This idea is rooted in his broader philosophy of language and communication, where he sees literature and narratives as forms of symbolic action that influence human behavior and thought. Burke saw storytelling as a fundamental human function that shapes perception, behavior, and social cohesion. It is not just entertainment but a mechanism of meaning-making, persuasion, and identity formation. Burke believed that stories function as guides for action. Whether in literature, religion, folklore, or daily conversation, narratives provide strategies for dealing with different life situations. They help people understand:

- How to react to conflicts
- How to handle success and failure
- How to relate to others (friends, enemies, authority figures)
- How to cope with uncertainty and crisis

For example, fables, myths, and parables often encode moral lessons and social norms, instructing individuals on what is considered good or bad behavior. Even modern stories—whether in movies, novels, or speeches—serve as templates for handling relationships, power struggles, and ethical dilemmas.

Burke saw different types of stories as strategies that reflect how individuals or societies approach specific problems. In his essay Literature as Equipment for Living, he explains that just as people develop practical tools to deal with physical challenges, they create narratives to cope with emotional and social challenges. He categorized literature and stories into different "proverbs" or "strategic responses" that provide frameworks for dealing with life.

- **Tragic narratives** help people process suffering and loss by showing how others have endured similar struggles.

- **Comedic stories** offer relief from hardship by allowing people to laugh at their problems and recognize human imperfections.

- **Epic and heroic tales** provide models of resilience, courage, and perseverance.

- **Satirical and critical narratives** expose hypocrisy and injustice, helping societies recognize and challenge systemic flaws.

Burke, Kenneth tied his idea of stories as "equipment for living" [4] to persuasion and rhetoric. He argued that all communication, including storytelling, is inherently persuasive because it invites people to adopt particular viewpoints and attitudes. By understanding the types of "equipment" stories provide, individuals can become more critical consumers of narratives and recognize the power dynamics behind them. In essence, storytelling is not just about entertainment — it is about survival, social cohesion, and personal meaning-making. Recognizing this allows us to engage more critically with the narratives we consume and create, ensuring that we use them wisely in shaping our lives.

In order to play all its power, the story needs to be believable, honest and beautiful. To do so, it needs to be well-constructed.

How to construct a story

Story is about change of the character. To make change meaningful you must express it and the audience must react to it in terms of value at stake. As Robert Mackee explained in his Book, STORY[3], Story values are the broadest sense of the idea, the soul of the story. Story Values are the universal qualities of human experience that my shift from positive to negative, or negative to positive, from moment to moment as: as love/hate, courage/cowardice, loyalty/betrayal, wisdom/stupidity…

A scene is an action through conflict in more or less continuous time and space that turns the value-charged condition of character's life on at least one value with the degree of perceptible significance?

Conflict should be as intense as possible. The protagonist and his story can only be as intellectually fascinating and emotionally as the forces of antagonism make them.

Human being is verry resourceful, verry inventive. They know how to multiply destructive power beyond the opposite charge of value and build a negative state that isn't just quantitatively worse, not just more and more of the same, but qualitatively worse, a darker intensity of a wholly new kind on a wholly scale. To take the story and character to the end of the line Robert Mckee[3] propose this technique:

- Beguin by identifying the primary value at stake in your story
- Identify the contradictory value, the direct opposite of the positive

- Between the positive and the negative is the contrary

- The contradictory is not the limit of human experience, at the end of the line waits the negation of the negation, a force of antagonism that is doubly negative

If story stops at the contradictory, or worse the contrary, it echoes the hundreds of mediocrities…For a story that is simply about love/hate, truth/lie, freedom/slavery, courage/cowardice, and the like is most certain to be trivial. If a story does not reach negation of the negation, it may strike the audience as satisfying but never brilliant, never sublime.

During the Climax, the protagonist's quest has carried him through the progressive complications until he has exhausted all actions to achieve his desire save one. Next action will be his last. He will be face to face with most focused powerful forces of antagonism. The crisis within the climax must be a true dilemma- a choice between irreconcilable goods, the lesser of two evils, or the two at once that place the protagonist under un intense pressure. The scene's climax should reveal the story most important value. At this crisis the protagonist makes a decision that takes him through a profound change. The protagonist decision should take into account, the value and most importantly what is important for the audience. The climax must be full of meaning. So, the audience will learn a great lesson.To do it great, the audience will have what it wants but not the way it expects.

The structure of the story

Myths are the cornerstones of each civilization, timeless stories that crystallize human experience, elevating it to a universal level. Imagine the Odyssey of Ulysses: this journey fraught with trials, temptations, and obstacles that, at every turn, echoes our own inner quest, our daily struggles. Myths remind us what it means to be human: to endure, to fail, to rise again, to persist.

The American mythologist Joseph Campbell[5], known for his work on comparative mythology and comparative religion, focused on the universal patterns and structures of myths, exploring how they shape human experience and understanding. Campbell described in his influential book "The Hero with a Thousand Faces" (1949) a common narrative structure that appears in the myths, legends, and stories of all cultures. This structure follows a hero who embarks on a transformative journey, faces trials, and ultimately returns transformed with new insights or powers. This model maps the universal stages a hero goes through, reflecting growth, transformation, and self-discovery. Today, superhero narratives inspire many Hollywood filmmakers and screenwriters. Their products are nothing other than modern myths, projections of our collective fears and hopes in an increasingly complex world. They fulfill the same ancestral role: to give shape to the inexplicable, to make the intangible tangible. A review of highly successful films reveals the adoption of the mythic narrative structure. A structure that has influenced humanity for centuries and continues to do so with the same force and breadth. When it comes to storytelling for management, the story needs to be as short as possible, as concise as possible. The simplified structure components are: The challenge, the descending crisis, the rock Bottom, the worst, the discovery, the rise, the return, the lesson. Since the story goal is to influence, it needs to finish with a call to action.

Engaging the audience, setting the tone of the story, suggesting its purpose from the very first lines, the story must captivate the audience, establishing a narrative pact where each word seems to echo the beating of their hearts. Picture a scene where twilight casts a purple hue over the outlines of an old town, where every step echoes against the worn cobblestones, carrying the echoes of a bygone era. The tone is set: melancholic, almost mythical, promising a quest that is both personal and universal. The goal? To traverse the shadows of humanity in search of the light of forgotten truths.

Providing context information without slowing down the pace the introduction of the world is done in subtle touches: an overheard conversation, faded posters on the walls, rumors of a looming revolt on the horizon. These details, naturally woven into the action, allow the setting to be built without hampering the pace of the story. We learn that the hero moves through a fractured society, on the brink of collapse, a world where grand ideologies clash and mingle in a chaotic dance.

The hero's internal and external problems the hero, for his part, is a mirror of this world: marked by invisible scars, he carries the weight of a tumultuous past and the fear of an uncertain future. Externally, the conflict is manifested by the threat of an imminent war, an oppressive power that grips like a vise. Internally, it is his battle against despair, his search for belonging and meaning in a world that seems to cruelly lack it.

The descending crisis

An external force that changes the course or intensity of the story: Here, the intervention of an external element acts as a catalyst for change. Imagine a sudden storm erupting during an important ceremony, forcing the protagonists to alter their plans. It is not merely the rain falling; it is fate, capriciously redirecting the aspirations and actions of the characters. Like a metaphor for life, these external forces remind us that control is often an illusion and that true mastery lies in our ability to navigate uncertainty.

An internal event can trigger the crossing of a threshold: Beyond external storms, there are internal tempests. A character may suddenly encounter a realization that upheaves their inner world. Take, for example, an unexpected betrayal that forces the hero to question their alliances and values. This moment of internal crisis is a threshold crossing, where the hero must decide to fight or flee, thus marking a point of no return in their personal journey.

The conjunction of the two: When external and internal forces combine, the effect on the hero is exponential. A hero may face an enemy while battling their own fears. This duality of conflicts creates a rich narrative tension that compels the character to either transcend or transform. It is in this forge that character is tempered, and true heroes emerge.

Putting the hero through a number of trials/Obstacles: Each obstacle is a trial by fire that shapes the hero. The trials vary in nature, some being physical, like crossing a scorching desert, others psychological, like overcoming the grief of a lost loved one. Each trial is a thread in the fabric of the story, reinforcing the overall pattern and deepening our connection with the hero. These obstacles are essential to prevent the narrative from stagnating and to maintain its momentum towards a resolution, often unexpected but inevitable.

The rock bottom

The "Mysterious Zone" is the space where the veil of the known dissolves, leaving the hero and the reader on the edge of a universe filled with uncertainties and possibilities. It is in this mist of the unknown that the narrative draws its strength, turning fear into a canvas on which the hero's greatest trials are outlined. This zone is not merely a geographical location but a state of mind where certainties crumble, and each step forward is an act of faith towards a still obscure resolution.

In this den of the unexplored, every shadow and every light that slips through the dense fog of possibilities can be a friend or foe. The hero, driven by fate or their own insatiable quest, must navigate this enigma, armed with courage yet vulnerable to the magnitude of what they do not yet know.

The Hero Develops Their Approach/Other Obstacles Advancing beyond the mysterious zone, the hero is compelled to refine or reinvent their approach to overcome obstacles that renew themselves or emerge with increased complexity. It is no longer just a battle against external foes but also an internal struggle to redefine their identity and convictions in the face of trials.

Each new challenge is a magnifying glass enlarging the hero's flaws and strengths. It is in this forge that resilience and perseverance are tempered. The hero, in developing their approach, does not merely adjust their strategies; they transform, learning from their mistakes, adapting to new realities, and sometimes accepting that victory requires unforeseen sacrifices.

Interacting with new allies or confronting more formidable opponents, each confrontation is a lesson, a step further towards the hero's maturity and the climax of the story. These renewed obstacles test not only their physical skills but also shake their ethics and motivations, pushing them towards deeper reflections on good, evil, and the cost of their ambitions.

The worst

In the narrative framework of any great story, the moment of "the worst" embodies the dramatic apex where the hero, confronted with his limits, is pushed to his last defenses. It is here that the hero faces not only his greatest challenge but also the most terrifying adversary. This duel often symbolizes an inner struggle, where the stakes surpass mere physical survival to touch the very essence of his being. The adversary, in this sense, can be a distorted reflection of the hero's deepest fears, thus providing a perfect canvas to paint his bravery and perseverance.

The hero's death is a powerful metaphor. He must die to be reborn; an idea found in many mythological traditions around the world. This "death" is not necessarily literal; it represents instead a complete abandonment of old ways of thinking and being, which no longer serve the hero's journey. In this crucible of despair, the hero frees himself from his invisible chains and emerges from his ashes, transformed and ready to embrace his new self with renewed vigor.

Upon returning changed, the hero embodies the truth that "the proximity of death makes life more real." This closeness to nothingness brings brutal clarity, a harsh contrast that enhances every joy, every pain, every moment of existence. The hero, having looked into the abyss, returns with a deeper appreciation of life, often accompanied by a wisdom that can only be acquired through trial.

Finally, this transformative journey leads the hero to focus on what is essential. Freed from the trivialities that once cluttered his mind, he can now clearly distinguish what is truly important. It is a purification of desires, a focus on what genuinely enriches existence, allowing the hero to continue his quest with a renewed sense of purpose and unwavering determination.

The discovery

In the narrative framework, the discovery is the critical moment where the hero, after enduring trials, faces the revelation of their journey. This moment is pivotal not only for the evolution of the story but also for the profound transformation of the character.

The hero will know the consequences of having lived: In the solitude of surmounted trials, the hero finds themselves shaped by opposing winds, with each challenge leaving an indelible mark on their being. Like a canvas painted in the tempests' wake, they observe the colors of their resilience and the shadows of their doubts. It is in this reflection that the hero realizes that each choice, each sacrifice, has been a stone laid on the path of their destiny. This moment of realization is often tinged with melancholy, but also gratitude, as these consequences are the silent witnesses of their transformation.

The hero seizes what they came for: Armed with new understanding, the hero finally grasps what they were destined to discover. Whether it be a new perception of themselves or the world, a clarity about the intentions of their heart, or a revelation that illuminates the shadowy areas of their journey, each element gathered is an invaluable treasure. This awakening is often depicted as a moment of blossoming where the hero finally sees themselves as they truly are, freed from illusions, ready to embrace their essence with brutal honesty. They stand at the peak of their own understanding, contemplating the horizon of possibilities that their trials have unlocked.

The hero is recognized and rewarded: Recognition, both internal and external, crowns the hero's journey. Other characters in the story, and sometimes the world itself, celebrate the hero's transformative return. This reward can take various forms—a leadership position, rediscovered love, or simply the inner peace and satisfaction of having accomplished what few would dare attempt. It is a tribute to the hero's perseverance and transformation, a celebration of the human spirit's endurance in the face of adversity. These stages of discovery, deeply embedded in the hero's journey cycle, reflect the universal steps of self-discovery and affirmation. The narrative takes on a philosophical dimension, inviting the reader to reflect on their own quest and the revelations of their journey.

The rise

In the dazzling light of triumph, the hero, once merely an echo in the tumult of the adventure, transforms into a legend. Recognition from his peers and the world around him is not just a reward materialized by laurels or treasures;

it is primarily a validation of his essence and his journey. This stage marks a rebirth, where endured sacrifices crystallize into an indelible aura that surrounds the hero. He becomes a symbol, an inspiration, a beacon whose brilliance guides lost souls towards bolder dreams."

Revelation, the keystone of all inner transformation, offers the hero an infinite palette of possibilities. Having deciphered the mysteries of a profound truth, he is now able to apply this newly acquired wisdom to greater, more complex challenges. Each choice, each action driven by this revelation strengthens his ability to influence, to transform the world according to this renewed vision. Thus, revelation becomes a compass that guides not only the hero but also those in his orbit, transforming lives and shaping destinies."

Making a choice: to stay in the ordinary world or remain in the extraordinary world"

"The conclusion of the epic leads the hero to a final and poignant dilemma: should he remain in this extraordinary world, forged by his exploits and trials, or return to the comforting banality of the ordinary world? This choice, far from trivial, reflects his inner quest. Staying in the extraordinary world means fully embracing the changes and continuing to live on the edge of the extraordinary. Returning to the ordinary world means accepting to resume an interrupted life, enriched and transformed, bearing new wisdom to share. It is a choice between two forms of peace: one found in acceptance, the other won in the perpetual quest.

The return

In the narrative arc of a story, the "return" phase is a pivotal moment where the hero, after undergoing trials and transformations, confronts his old world, armed with new perspectives and abilities. This stage unfolds in three essential points.

Purging the Past/Catharsis: The hero's return is marked by significant purification. Having faced challenges that pushed him to his limits, he emerges leaving behind the doubts and fears that hindered him. This process of purgation is not merely psychological but is manifested in his actions and choices. It represents a catharsis where the hero frees himself from the slag of the past to reveal a more refined essence, ready to reintegrate into the fabric of his original world. This transformation is often symbolized by acts of renunciation or reconciliation with figures from the past, thus illustrating a definitive break from old shackles.

Demonstrating Character Change/A New Personality: The returning hero is no longer the person who left home. This point is crucial in the narrative, as it illustrates the character's internal metamorphosis. The change can be subtle or radical, but it is always definitive. This new self is often characterized by increased maturity, newly acquired wisdom, or a changed outlook on life.

Testing Ground for New Skills: Finally, the return serves as a proving ground for the skills and knowledge acquired during the adventure. The familiar world of the hero, with its known challenges, provides an ideal setting to put these new abilities into practice. Whether it's resolving lingering conflicts, innovating a traditional practice, or positively transforming the community, the hero concretely demonstrates the extent of his growth. It would be better to render this demonstration vibrant and tangible, infusing these moments with dramatic intensity that underscores the hero's evolution and the impact of his new skills on his surroundings.

As we weave the threads of our stories, each fragment carries an emotional charge that culminates in what is called "the lesson."

Another Experience Similar to the Extreme Trial: Every powerful narrative often begins with a challenge, a hurdle that the protagonist must overcome. Revisiting a similar ordeal offers the reader a window into the hero's past, illuminating their deep motivations and resilience in the face of adversity. This repetition of trials is not merely a return but an ascending spiral, where each confrontation both reflects and revises the past, thus forging an indelible link between the character and their audience.

Demonstrating Success/Celebration: The celebration is the climax where the narrative tension is released, and the hero, and by extension the reader, can finally breathe and relish the victory. The success is not only that of the protagonist but also of the reader who has journeyed through the story. It is a moment of sharing, a communion between the storyteller and their audience. The joy is all the more palpable because it is shared, transforming words into a collective and memorable experience.

Catharsis: In the Aristotelian tradition, catharsis represents the purification of emotions. It is at the heart of modern narration. After the storm of conflicts and the joy of victory comes the calm of catharsis. Here, the narrative resonates with our own lives, allowing us to let go, to free ourselves from our own burdens through empathy and reflection. It is a moment where the narrative prompts us to question ourselves, to reflect on our own experiences, and to draw universal lessons.

Call to action

The "call to action" (CTA) at the end of a short story can be a powerful tool for engaging readers, prompting them to think, feel, or act in a specific way after finishing the story. This technique is often used in marketing, advocacy, and persuasive writing but can be creatively adapted to narrative fiction to enhance the story's impact or extend its message beyond the page.

In narrative terms, a CTA is not just about selling or convincing; it's about urging the audience to consider something deeply, change their perspective, or undertake a specific action inspired by the themes or implications of the story. This can be achieved through a direct appeal from the narrator or characters, or more subtly through the plot's resolution and final lines.

Its purpose is to encourage audience to reflect on their own lives, beliefs, or actions, generate a strong emotional response that compels them to share their feelings about the story with others and motivate them to change their behavior or undertake an activity that aligns with the story's message.

Asking a series of questions about the hero Who is he really? A rebel, a sage, a madman? What motivates him to get up every morning? What are the wounds that are not visible to the naked eye? Is he a hero by choice or by circumstance? These questions, posed as challenges to the reader, invite them to dive deeper into the psyche of the character, making him more real, more tangible.

Fostering identification with the hero Finally, for identification with the hero to occur, he must expose his vulnerabilities, his doubts. When he shares his most intimate thoughts, his deepest fears, the reader, moved, sees themselves in him. It is in this shared humanity, these moments of weakness, that the hero becomes someone to root for, someone we hope to see triumph, because through his struggle, it is somewhat our own that we are fighting.

In the realm of creative writing, the concept that "the story is never perfect, never finished" resonates deeply with both novice and experienced writers. This idea parallels the principle of prototyping used in design and technology fields, where initial models are continuously refined through iterations based on testing and feedback. Applying the prototyping approach to storytelling can greatly enhance the development and enrichment of narratives.

The process of constructing a story

Beside all what is described above. I share with you my experience as author. I use two ways to concretely build a story. Sometimes both of them. I could call them Down up and Top Down, depending on the information availability and the imagination clarity. It is my way to fight the white page syndrome.

Structure what we know (Down up)

Decide on the specific theme you want to explore through storytelling. Start by choosing a clear and focused theme that you are passionate about or that holds significance for you or your intended audience. This theme will guide the development of your story and ensure that all elements contribute towards a unified message. Consider themes that evoke universal emotions or connect with broad or specific audiences. The theme could range from personal growth and overcoming adversity to improving productivity, building capabilities, or discovery.

Gather any relevant information or descriptions of experiences, either your own or those of someone you know, that relate to your chosen theme. Compile detailed accounts of experiences that directly tie into your theme. These can be personal anecdotes, historical events, or narratives you've heard from others that resonate with the central motif of your story. Pay attention to collecting diverse perspectives and rich details that paint a vivid picture of the setting, characters, and events.

For each element of your story's structure, collect pertinent details. Break down your story into its structural components specified. For each section, identify and collect specific details that advance the plot and develop the characters. Ensure that each segment logically flows into the next, building tension and interest as the story progresses towards its climax.

Emphasize and enhance the experiential aspects to amplify emotional impact. Focus on the sensory and emotional details that make your story come alive. Use descriptive language to evoke sights, sounds, smells, and tactile experiences. Highlight emotional shifts and reactions to develop a deeper connection with the audience. The goal is to make the audience feel the emotions experienced by the characters through well-crafted narrative techniques.

Organize all the information into a compelling narrative, ensuring it aligns with the elements outlined above. This could involve adhering to specific storytelling frameworks or narrative theories that are effective for your genre or medium. Ensure that each element from your collected data serves the story's overall arc and helps to reinforce your central theme.

Share your initial draft with someone to obtain feedback, or set it aside for a while and revisit it later for revision. After drafting your story, it's beneficial to get external feedback to refine and enhance your narrative. Share your draft with trusted peers, mentors, or a writing group, and be open to constructive criticism. Alternatively, leave your draft for a period of time—this distance can provide new perspectives and insights when you return to it. Use this feedback and your revised thoughts to polish and perfect the narrative, ensuring it resonantly delivers the intended message and emotional impact.

Decompose from what we would like to be (Up Down)

Decide on the main theme you want to focus on in your storytelling. Start by identifying the central theme that will anchor your storytelling. This theme should resonate deeply with both you and your audience, and it should be broad enough to explore through various angles yet specific enough to provide a focused narrative. Consider what you are most passionate about or a unique insight you have that others may find enlightening.

Reflect on a profound experience that taught you a valuable lesson you wish to share with stakeholders. Think about a significant event or series of events in your life that had a lasting impact on you. This experience should be one that brought about a profound understanding or a shift in perspective. Reflect on how this event shaped your personal or professional life and why its lessons are valuable to your stakeholders.

Begin by recalling the sequence of actions and decisions that led to this experience, detailing each step. Map out the timeline of events that led to the pivotal experience. Detail the decisions you made and the actions you took that contributed to the outcome. This step is crucial as it sets the stage for the narrative, providing a clear path that led to the lessons learned.

Be precise in explaining the reasons and methods involved. As you narrate each step, clarify why you made certain decisions and how you executed specific actions. This clarity will not only enhance the storytelling by adding depth to the narrative, but it will also help your audience understand the logic and emotions driving your decisions at the time.

Arrange all decisions and actions according to the framework outlined above. This framework might suggest arranging your narrative chronologically, thematically, or in order of importance. Adhering to a structured approach helps in maintaining a coherent and logical flow, making the story easier for the audience to follow and absorb.

Craft all the information into an engaging narrative that adheres to the elements outlined above, creating the initial draft. With all the details at hand and a framework to guide you, begin drafting your story. Integrate the key to create a compelling narrative. Ensure that your story is engaging, emotionally resonant, and aligns with the intended message and lessons you wish to convey.

Share the draft with someone to gather feedback, or set it aside for a while and revisit it later for revisions. Once your initial draft is complete, consider sharing it with a trusted colleague, mentor, or friend who can provide constructive feedback. An outside perspective can offer insights that you might have overlooked and suggest improvements that can enhance the narrative. Alternatively, setting the draft aside for a period can give you a fresh perspective when you return to it, allowing you to refine and polish the narrative with a clear mind.

Continuous improving

A story, much like a prototype, is a draft—a form still in evolution. Every story begins as a rough sketch of ideas and evolves through multiple drafts and revisions. The essence of storytelling is not to achieve perfection on the first try but to develop the narrative incrementally, enhancing its depth, clarity, and impact with each iteration. This process acknowledges that a story can always be improved and adapted to better meet the needs of its audience or to deepen its thematic explorations.

In creative writing, adopting the mindset that a story is "never perfect, never finished" is not a sign of weakness but a testament to the fluid and evolving nature of art. Stories, much like prototypes, are iterative by nature. They grow and improve over time, shaped by feedback and the writer's evolving insights. This approach does not just apply to individual stories but also to the craft of writing as a whole, where each story written is a step in the ongoing journey of mastering narrative creation. By embracing this process, writers can continue to refine their skills, expand their creative horizons, and enrich the literary landscape with ever more compelling narratives.

How to adapt and create your own story

Insightful points	Your story
Look for your professional experiences that led you or someone else further to the negation of the negation	•
Remember one experience when you or someone else have been, put on a crisis: a true dilemma- a choice between irreconcilable goods, the lesser of two evils	•
Remember when you or someone else have made a decision based on an important value	•
Remember an experience that has changed you or someone else intensely	•
Construct a story based on the point above or part of them	•

Takeaways

- Story is about change of the character
- Story Values are the universal qualities of human experience that my shift from positive to negative, or negative to positive
- Story values are the broadest sense of the idea, the soul of the story.
- The crisis within the climax must be a true dilemma- a choice between irreconcilable goods, the lesser of two evils, or the two at once that place the protagonist under un intense pressure
- The protagonist decision should take into account, the value and most importantly what is important for the audience
- The story should go as long as possible near the negation of the negation, a force of antagonism that is doubly negative

How to improve the story

We could use the Iterative Process of Story Development as follows:

Initial Drafting: The first draft of a story is equivalent to a basic prototype. It lays down the foundation and structure, allowing the writer to pour out ideas without concern for flaws or inconsistencies. This stage is crucial for creativity, as it captures the raw essence of the narrative.

Feedback Integration: Just as a prototype is tested and reviewed, a story benefits immensely from feedback. Writers often share drafts with peers, editors, or beta readers to gain insights and perspectives that are not visible from the author's vantage point. This feedback is invaluable for identifying weak points, gaps, or elements that may not resonate with readers.

Revisions and Refinement: With feedback in hand, the story undergoes revisions—sometimes minor adjustments, sometimes major overhauls. Each revision is aimed at enhancing character development, plot coherence, thematic depth, and emotional impact, much like refining a prototype to improve its functionality and design.

Continuous Improvement: Even after publication, a story can continue to evolve. Authors might revisit their narratives in subsequent editions, or adapt them into different media such as films or plays, each time viewing the story through a new lens and making adjustments based on changing contexts or deeper understanding.

PART II: PROJECT MANAGEMENT PROCESSES AND STORYTELLING

127

V.   Project processes groups and storytelling

Story: Never make a case for what can't be defended

Karim was tasked with directing a substantial research and development project – a challenge not only of technical scope but also of strategic significance, aimed at evaluating the impact of a new technology on the workings of the organization. This project was poised to shape the technological trajectory of the company and required the engagement of numerous stakeholders, each advocating for their preferred vision of the technology to be tested, thus influencing the choice of market segment and geographic focus.

Karim, as competent as he was unwaveringly honest – his candor verging on naivety – had carefully selected Area A as the most promising location for deploying and capitalizing on this new technology. However, at the project's outset, external pressures swayed the steering committee, redirecting the focus to Area B, which preliminary studies had deemed less promising.

As the project unfolded, Karim's concerns were validated: the results were inconclusive, leading to criticism and disillusionment among other stakeholders, who perceived it as a blatant failure. Karim faced criticism for allegedly failing to sufficiently advocate for the insights of his preliminary study. In an ironic twist, the influential member who had redirected the project to Area B gained further influence and ascended to the presidency of the steering committee, joining those who critiqued and overturned the project's original decisions.

Furthermore, this individual demanded that Karim provide justifications for the decisions that led to the project's downfall, forcing him into the untenable position of defending a course of action he had never endorsed. These were among the most challenging days of his career. Yet, from this trial, Karim derived a crucial lesson: the importance of grounding decisions in robust analysis, defending them assertively, and resisting the sway of even the most powerful stakeholders if it threatens the project's success. Now fortified by this experience, he resolved to develop a resilience to undue influence, building a defense against those who, whether through intent or oversight, disregard the collective success.

Have you ever encountered a similar situation? What was your reaction? And how would you handle it if it occurred again?

Background of using storytelling and during project Management Processes Groups

From the story told earlier, a subtle lesson emerges — almost whispered to those who know how to listen: it's not enough to master the art of influencing stakeholders. One must also cultivate an inner vigilance, a sharp clarity, to resist the influence of others — especially when their intentions stray from the project's true path. For while some seek to make an impact, others seek to impose one. And if we don't forge within ourselves a strategic immunity, we may find ourselves unknowingly carrying the colors of an agenda that isn't ours. Influence, yes... but without being swept away.

The Illusion of Innocent Stories: Every narrative, regardless of its simplicity, carries with it potent undercurrents that shape perceptions and ideologies. Far from being mere recitations of events, stories actively forge cultural and personal identities. This influence elevates storytellers from entertainers to powerful shapers of society.

Emotional Packaging of Ideas: Stories uniquely entwine their central ideas with emotions, making them more than intellectual pursuits. This emotional packaging enables stories to bypass rational barriers and embed ideas deep within the audience's subconscious. Consequently, stories are not just processed intellectually; they are experienced emotionally, ensuring that their messages resonate deeply and enduringly.

The Ethical Weight of Influence: The ability to implant ideas through storytelling carries with it significant ethical responsibility. Narratives can subtly manipulate thoughts and sway public opinion, thereby shaping societal values and individual behaviors. As such, storytellers must wield their influence with care and integrity, mindful of the impact their narratives may have on diverse audiences.

Strategic Storytelling for Effective Decision-Making: In strategic contexts, the selection of stories should be purposefully aligned with the objectives at hand. Effective storytelling can illuminate complex issues, guiding stakeholders toward clearer, more informed decision-making. By carefully crafting narratives that underscore crucial facts and potential outcomes, storytellers can ensure that decisions contribute positively to the success of projects or initiatives. This targeted approach maximizes the potential of storytelling to influence outcomes beneficially.

How storytelling can be integrated into each process group of the project lifecycle can provide a deeper understanding of its practical applications. Let's delve deeper into each process group[1] with more detailed examples and approaches:

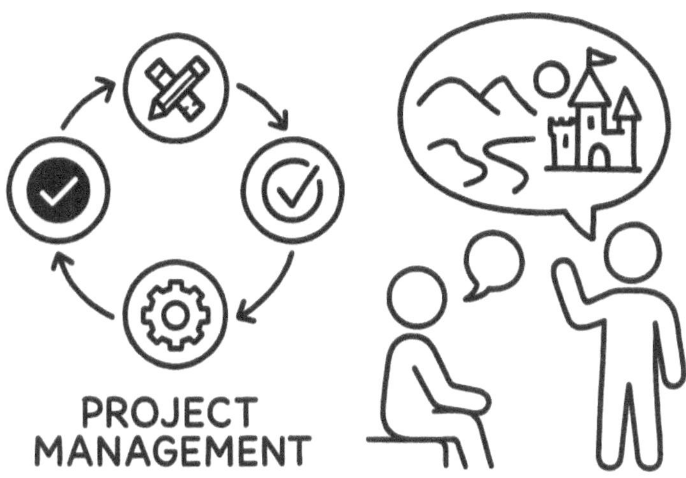

Fig. 5 Storytelling and Project Management Processes

Initiation processes

In the Initiation process, the project is defined and authorized. Storytelling at this stage should focus on creating a vivid narrative that connects emotionally with stakeholders. For example, you could tell the story of a day in the life of an end user before and after the project's completion, illustrating the struggles they currently face and how the project will alleviate these pains. This story can be based on real testimonials or hypothetical scenarios that highlight the direct benefits of the project. Use this narrative in initial presentations to sponsors and stakeholders to foster an emotional investment that supports project approval.

Planning processes

During the Planning process, storytelling can help in visualizing the project's path and potential hurdles. Consider using historical analogies or success stories from similar projects within the organization or industry. For instance, narrate how a previous project's meticulous resource allocation model led to its success, and how you plan to adopt a similar model tailored to the current project's specifics. Use these stories in team meetings and documentation to help stakeholders understand the planning logic, thereby facilitating clearer and more informed decision-making.

Execution processes

As the project moves into the Execution, maintaining team morale and motivation is critical. Storytelling can play a key role in highlighting individual or team contributions that had a significant impact on past projects. Share stories that focus on problem-solving, innovation, and teamwork, emphasizing how these behaviors positively influenced the project outcomes. This not only serves to motivate the team but also sets behavioral expectations. Additionally, celebrate small wins through stories in regular updates or meetings to keep the team engaged and focused.

Monitoring and Controlling processes

Monitoring and Controlling processes require constant adjustment and realignment. Storytelling can be used to frame the adjustments as opportunities for innovation rather than setbacks. Share narratives about past projects where adaptive changes led to better-than-expected outcomes. For example, a story where unexpected supplier issues led the team to find a more efficient alternative that not only saved cost but also improved the product's quality. These stories can help in cultivating a resilient and agile project culture that views challenges as opportunities.

For Closing processes it's important to consolidate the project's achievements and lessons. Create a comprehensive story that encompasses the entire project lifecycle, highlighting how each phase contributed to the project's success. Include testimonials from beneficiaries, team members, and stakeholders that speak to the project's impact. This narrative can be presented in a final report or a celebratory closure meeting. It serves not only as a project summary for documentation purposes but also as a tool for reflecting on what was achieved and what could be improved for future projects.

By deeply embedding storytelling into each processes Group, project managers can more effectively communicate complex information, manage stakeholder expectations, motivate teams, and document project history and achievements in a way that is engaging and meaningful. This approach not only aids in the immediate project's success but also contributes to organizational learning and future project planning.

How to adapt and create your own story

Story components	Your own story
Recall an experience where you (or someone you know) needed to be aware of a stakeholder's influence.	
Remember a time when you were influenced by a key stakeholder to make a decision against your better judgment, only to discover later that it did not contribute to the success of the project.	
What were the consequences of that decision?	
Have you ever experienced a situation where you faced "the negation of the negation "that led to further complications? How did that make you feel?	
How did you resolve the issue?	
What would you have done differently?	
What did you learn from the whole experience?	
Imagine you are faced with the same situation again. What preparations would you need to make?	
Construct a narrative using the elements above.	
Share it with someone to give you feedback.	

Takeaways

- Storytelling can be integrated into each process group of the project lifecycle
- Complex project with many stakes, requiring multiple perspectives; a single perspective is never enough.
- Each stakeholder could not only be engaged but also influence, and why not using storytelling with the project manager?
- It's more beneficial to promote diversity.
- The importance of the project, its outcomes, and benefits in decision-making.
- What is important to the stakeholders?
- The project manager might personally experience a situation where they face "the negation of the negation."
- The project manager themselves could be influenced.
- To influence is first and foremost to be honest.

How to improve and sharpen your story

Harnessing the Power of Anecdotes in Storytelling. Anecdotes are powerful storytelling tools that have captivated audiences from time immemorial. They serve as windows into the world of the speaker, offering personal glimpses that resonate deeply with listeners. By integrating anecdotes into storytelling, the narrator achieves a connection that is not only intellectual but also profoundly emotional. This narrative technique is particularly effective because it transforms abstract concepts into tangible experiences that listeners can relate to and reflect upon.

Anecdotes function as the narrative equivalent of prisms, bending the light of the storyteller's experience through a spectrum that is uniquely human and universally relatable. Consider, for instance, the impact of a business leader sharing a personal story of failure and resilience. This narrative could begin with a vivid recounting of a specific moment when everything seemed lost—an unexpected market downturn, a critical error in judgment, or a venture that fell apart despite best efforts. The details of these experiences, when articulated well, do more than convey facts; they paint a picture that draws the audience into the moment of crisis.

The true power of an anecdote emerges in its capacity to push the audience towards reflection. After sharing an intense personal story, a skilled storyteller will often transition to posing reflective questions to the audience: "Have you ever faced a moment like this? What did you learn from it?" This technique invites the listener to delve into their reservoir of experiences, find parallels, and derive personal insights. It's not just a passive listening exercise but an active engagement that encourages introspection and self-evaluation.

Moreover, anecdotes are invaluable for their versatility. They can be seamlessly woven into speeches, presentations, educational materials, or even casual conversations. Each context might demand a different tone or style, ranging from humorous to solemn, but the core objective remains the same: to convey a message in a way that sticks with the audience long after the story is told.

Effective storytelling with anecdotes also involves a sense of timing and relevance. The anecdote must not only be interesting but also aptly placed to enhance the narrative's overall impact. It should serve as a bridge, connecting the narrative's various elements and reinforcing the story's theme. For instance, in a discussion about the importance of adaptability in business, a well-chosen anecdote about a last-minute pivot that led to unexpected success can illustrate the point more vividly than any abstract argument.

The art of storytelling is significantly enhanced by the use of anecdotes. These personal stories bring color and depth to narratives, making abstract concepts concrete and stimulating reflective thinking. As storytellers harness this tool, they do more than share information; they forge emotional connections and foster a shared space of understanding and insight. Whether in a boardroom, a classroom, or around a campfire, anecdotes are a storyteller's ally, making every tale not just told but truly felt.

VI.   Initiating processes

Story: An unimplemented good idea becomes a challenge for the future.

Hamid, the CEO of a research and development firm, was charged with crafting a robust knowledge management system. His mission? To establish a repository where all ideas, detailed with their insights and learned lessons, would be stored to leverage these assets for significantly boosting productivity by saving time and resources. Despite the pressing need for this initiative, Hamid remained skeptical, torn between other priorities and his belief that idea exchanges would be more effective if conducted directly among experts.

During a routine quarterly meeting, however, he was shocked to find that concepts previously debated by his teams were resurfacing in new projects. Alarmed, he established an inspection commission to delve into these discrepancies. The investigation's outcomes were illuminating: over 30% of the ideas were routinely recycled and touted as new, even forming the cornerstone of the strategic plan for the upcoming four years that he had personally endorsed.

The response from the idea managers to this audit was icy, perceived as a witch hunt. They further revealed that the other 70% were merely old ideas repackaged. Confronted with this disclosure, Hamid realized that his lack of reliable information was hindering his ability to make well-informed decisions.

In response, a freshly recruited young employee suggested reviving a previously unexecuted concept: the systematic preservation of ideas and the learnings from each project. "This was a proposal once set aside, and one that we deeply regret overlooking," Hamid admitted. Implementing such a system would have enhanced the filtering, ranking, and refinement of ideas over time, elevating their success potential and bolstering the company's reputation among shareholders.

Hamid appointed the new hire to spearhead this initiative and required other innovators to produce a comparative analysis of their projects against the archived ideas. Thanks to the COVID-19 pandemic, which had necessitated remote collaboration, the teams had proven their capacity to operate effectively without direct physical interactions. Inspired by these developments, Hamid made this insight his motto: "An unimplemented good idea becomes a challenge for the future." What are your thoughts on this perspective?

How to use storytelling during the initiation process

From the story just told, a gentle yet unshakable truth emerges: even the brightest idea will only bloom in fertile ground. A seed, no matter how noble its nature, only becomes a tree if the soil welcomes it, if the season embraces it, if the sky offers its rain. So, it is with projects — being right is not enough; timing must also be right — that fleeting window when the winds shift in your favor. Only then can a genuine story of influence take root, anchored in the right conditions, capable of gaining support without ever forcing fate.

The most important and specific axes to use the storytelling during the initiation are below.

- Craft a compelling story that outlines the origins of the project, the core problem it aims to solve, and the envisioned future once the project is completed.
- Project Manager or Sponsor story to highlight his competencies and success stories before the project.
- Organization Story to highlight its assets and decision-making approach success stories to inspire stakeholders.

In project management, particularly during the initiation phase, storytelling can be a powerful tool to engage and align stakeholders. Here's how a well-crafted story can be structured to capture the essence of a project effectively:

Fig.6 Storytelling during the initiation processes

Origins of the Project: The story begins by setting the stage for why the project exists in the first place. This involves a clear, engaging narrative that details the circumstances and insights that led to the identification of the need for the project. For instance, a company might have noticed a significant gap in their product offerings compared to market demands through customer feedback and competitor analysis. This part of the story not only contextualizes the project within real-world observations but also connects emotionally with stakeholders by highlighting the thorough groundwork and strategic thinking that underpin the project's genesis.

The Core Problem It Aims to Solve: This segment of the story dives into the specifics of the challenges or problems the project intends to address. It articulates the issues in a way that resonates with the stakeholders' interests and concerns, making the problem palpable and urgent. For example, if the project aims to develop a new software tool, the story would illustrate how current solutions are inadequate, perhaps by showcasing real-life frustrations or inefficiencies experienced by users. This narrative piece not only defines the scope of the problem but also builds a case for why the project's goals are both valuable and necessary, fostering a sense of shared urgency among stakeholders.

The Envisioned Future Once the Project is Completed: The final part of the story casts a vision for the future, describing what success looks like and how it changes the current scenario. This forward-looking perspective should paint a vivid picture of the benefits and improvements post-project completion, encompassing both tangible outcomes like increased efficiency or revenue, and intangible benefits like enhanced customer satisfaction or employee morale. By illustrating the positive transformations expected from the project, this narrative helps stakeholders visualize the strategic impact and potential return on investment, thereby generating excitement and buy-in.

In using storytelling this way, the project manager not only informs but also inspires stakeholders by framing the project as a journey worth embarking on together. This approach not only ensures that the importance and relevance of the project are understood but also helps in building a strong foundational support amongst all involved parties from the very outset.

Another effective strategy for achieving this engagement is through the use of storytelling, particularly stories that highlight the competencies and success of the project manager or sponsor. This approach not only captivates the audience but also strategically aligns their expectations and support for the project. Here's a deeper look at the benefits of this storytelling approach:

Building Trust and Credibility: Crafting a story that showcases the project manager or sponsor's competencies and past successes serves as a powerful tool to build trust among stakeholders. When stakeholders hear about the concrete achievements and the challenges previously overcome by the project leaders, they are more likely to develop confidence in the leader's abilities to steer the new project to success. This trust is fundamental, especially in the initial stages of the project, where uncertainty can be high, and stakeholder buy-in is essential.

Creating a Personal Connection: A well-told story does more than just relay facts; it weaves these facts into a narrative that resonates on a personal level with its audience. By highlighting personal anecdotes or significant milestones in the project manager's career, the story helps stakeholders see beyond the professional veneer. This personal connection is crucial as it humanizes the project leader, making stakeholders more empathetic and supportive of the project's goals. It underscores the leader's commitment and passion, which are contagious qualities that can motivate stakeholders to align their efforts with the project objectives.

Setting the Tone for the Project's Vision and Goals: The story of a competent and successful leader sets a positive tone for the project. It acts as a live demonstration of the project manager's capability and sets a benchmark for what the stakeholders can expect. Moreover, this storytelling approach can be strategically used to bridge the past successes of the project leader with the potential and vision of the current project. Stakeholders are presented with a narrative that not only highlights past achievements but also aligns them with the future aspirations of the project, thereby making the project's goals seem more attainable and exciting.

Using storytelling to showcase the project manager or sponsor's competencies and success stories in the initiation phase of project management is a powerful engagement strategy. It builds trust, creates a personal connection, and sets a positive, aspirational tone for the project. This narrative technique not only ensures that stakeholders are engaged and supportive but also fosters an environment where the project's objectives are clearly understood and enthusiastically embraced.

In the initiation phase of project management, the strategic use of storytelling can be a powerful tool to engage stakeholders effectively. Crafting a compelling organizational success story that highlights its assets and decision-making approach serves three pivotal functions: it inspires stakeholders, underscores the organization's competencies, and aligns stakeholder expectations with project goals.

A well-crafted success story serves as a beacon of inspiration for stakeholders. By presenting a narrative that showcases past successes, the organization doesn't just recount what has been achieved but also energizes stakeholders about what's possible. This emotional engagement is crucial because it transforms the stakeholders from passive observers into active participants who are emotionally invested in the success of the new project. Inspirational stories can drive enthusiasm and commitment, which are essential for the long-term sustainability of the project.

An organization's success story is fundamentally a showcase of its assets and competencies. By articulating how the organization has effectively utilized its resources in the past to overcome challenges and achieve goals, the story acts as a proof of capability. This not only builds credibility in the eyes of stakeholders but also instills confidence in the organization's operational and strategic capabilities. For new projects, this means stakeholders are more likely to trust the organization's ability to manage and utilize resources efficiently, reducing resistance and fostering a smoother project initiation.

Aligning Stakeholder Expectations with Project Goals: Effective storytelling ensures that the stakeholders' expectations are aligned with the project's goals from the outset. By using a narrative that integrates the organization's strategic objectives with its achievements, stakeholders can see the direct benefits of their involvement and support. This alignment is critical in mitigating misunderstandings and misalignments that can derail projects. Furthermore, it helps in setting realistic expectations, thereby providing a clear roadmap for stakeholders to visualize their roles and the potential impact of the project.

The strategic use of storytelling in project management, especially during the initiation phase, is more than just an engagement tactic; it is a foundational strategy that inspires, demonstrates capability, and aligns goals. By effectively employing storytelling, project managers can set the stage for successful project execution and stakeholder satisfaction.

How to adapt and create your own story

Insightful points	Your story
Decide on the main theme related to project initiation you want to focus on in your storytelling.	•
Reflect on a profound experience that taught you (or someone you know) a valuable lesson about how to engage stakeholders during initiation process.	•
Describe and amplify how actions and decisions were made during that experience, before and after.	•
Construct a story based on the points above	•
Share it with someone to give you feedback.	•

Takeaways

- Craft a compelling story that outlines the origins of the project, the core problem it aims to solve, and the envisioned future once the project is completed.
- Project Manager or Sponsor story to highlight his competencies and success stories before the project.
- Organization Story to highlight its assets and decision-making approach success stories to inspire stakeholders.

What could be more impactful, project manager story, sponsor story, organization story or both?

Creating a story specific to project is fundamental in a way that it help to create focus and the project result create a constant reminder of the project goal. So, story about it is very helpful. The points specified above are proposed axes according to our experiences and exchange with several project managers who have experienced challenges and storytelling has helped them. As all we know, every project has its own challenges, so you could focus on a specific problem and build your own story. Stories described in this book could be used as inspiration material.

How can you enhance your story by tailoring your language to your audience?

Imagine you are presenting a project to create a new product/service/solution to a group of stakeholders. Among them, you have visual, auditory, and kinesthetic learners. To engage each of them effectively, you could weave a narrative that appeals to these distinct sensory channels.

Visual: Begin by painting a vivid picture of the scenario. Describe the sleek design of the product, its vibrant colors, and its placement in a bright, modern setting. Use phrases like "Imagine seeing this elegant design as a centerpiece of your living room, its surfaces gleaming under the soft light." This creates a strong image in the minds of visual-oriented people, who tend to think and learn best through pictures and spatial understanding.

Auditory: Introduce the auditory elements by describing the subtle sounds associated with the product. For example, if it's a high-tech gadget, mention the soft, reassuring beeps it emits when operational or the satisfying click of a well-engineered button. Use rhythmic, melodic language to appeal to those who appreciate sounds, such as "Listen to the symphony of soft clicks and whirrs that affirm its precision engineering."

Kinesthetic: To engage kinesthetic learners, who feel more connected through touch and movement, describe the texture of the product's materials, the weight of it in one's hands, or even the sensation of using it. Phrases like "Feel the cool, smooth metal against your skin and the lightweight balance that makes it easy to handle" can effectively draw in those who relate best to tactile experiences.

By integrating these sensory details into your narrative, you provide a holistic experience that appeals to the varied sensory preferences of your audience. This method not only enriches the storytelling but also enhances comprehension and retention, making your presentation more impactful and memorable.

VII.   Project Planning

Story: Do not solidify the mutable, nor animate the immutable

Sara, the CEO of an organization dedicated to the enhancement and marketing of natural products, was overseeing a major project: the construction of a cobalt processing plant, intended to enrich cathodes for electric vehicle batteries. In the market, two technologies predominated: LFP and LMC, with the latter initially having the advantage.

However, as time — the unforgiving arbiter — passed, it revealed a growing inclination among automakers for the LFP technology, attracted by its more affordable cost despite its lower energy density. This trend threatened to undermine the very foundations of Sara's multi-year project. A major risk emerged: the possibility of irrevocably missing the window of opportunity.

Faced with a potential financial abyss, and with limited resources to embark on a similar project, the future of the organization seemed to wobble. In this precarious context, a decision was made: to launch a study to assess the feasibility of adapting the process or, failing that, to pivot towards producing other minerals such as iron or manganese, which might capture a market if LFP dominated.

The study concluded that such an adaptation would be difficult. The best strategy was to accelerate the project to seize, even partially, the opportunity and minimize losses.

In a spirit of introspection, a review of the initial assumptions was undertaken, revealing misconceptions about the stability of cobalt prices and the evolution of the market, which was not subject to a fixed technological standard. During the presentation of this analysis, Sara shared an enlightening anecdote to inspire her team:

One evening, a traveler arrived in a village during the night of the 26th of Ramadan. Upon entering the mosque, he was greeted by a feast of couscous and various juices. Delighted, he anticipated an even more lavish night to follow. To his dismay, he found the mosque closed the next night, unaware that the 26th of Ramadan was a specific celebration. This episode led him to advocate for a rigorous system of belief and hypothesis testing, emphasizing the importance of relying on verifiable facts and methodically planning their examination.

Since then, he adopted the maxim: "Do not solidify the mutable, nor animate the immutable."

In what context might you consider using this maxim?

How to use storytelling during the project planning Process

"This episode led him to advocate for a rigorous system of belief and hypothesis testing, emphasizing the importance of relying on verifiable facts and methodically planning their examination." This the great lesson from the above story.

As previously mentioned in the initiation process group, one truth remains: any story worth telling can only take root in well-prepared soil. It's not enough to simply tell a story; it must first be grounded. Planning—this forward-facing gaze toward the horizon—is not fueled by certainty alone. It moves cautiously, drawing on facts, yes, but also on assumptions—those sketches of a future not yet seen.

So, when the goal is to convince stakeholders, it's no longer just about lining up rational arguments. You must build a narrative. A narrative that gives meaning to the chosen path, that unites, that rallies. Because it's not the plan itself that drives action—it's the meaning behind it. And that's where storytelling becomes both weapon and compass, aligning scattered intentions toward a shared direction.

Below are potential areas where we could apply storytelling during project planification

- Develop narratives that improve decision making
- Use storytelling to explore different scheduling scenarios and their potential impacts on project outcomes
- Use storytelling to explore different scenarios (make or buy) and their potential impacts on project outcomes
- Create character-driven stories to highlight the roles and responsibilities of key project team members
- Develop narratives that describe potential risks and their impact through hypothetical scenarios

Storytelling is an invaluable tool in the project planning process, enhancing clarity, engagement, and foresight among project teams. Here's how storytelling can be effectively integrated into different aspects of project planning in more detailed description.

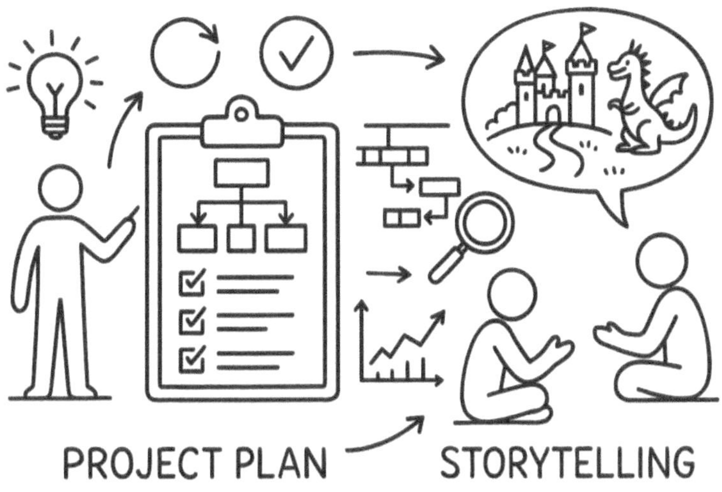

Fig.7 Using Storytelling during planification processes

Develop narratives that improve decision making: Crafting stories around past projects or hypothetical situations can provide powerful insights for decision making. By presenting a narrative that includes the problem, the steps taken, and the outcomes achieved, team members can visualize the decision-making process more clearly. For example, a story might detail how a previous project overcame budget constraints by prioritizing essential tasks, guiding current decisions on budget allocation and resource prioritization.

Use storytelling to explore different scheduling scenarios and their potential impacts on project outcomes: Narratives can be constructed to simulate the effects of different scheduling choices. For instance, a story could depict a scenario where a project is accelerated, outlining potential benefits such as beating competitors to market, alongside risks like increased costs or compromised quality. Conversely, another story might explore the impact of extending the project timeline, allowing for more thorough testing and refinement but risking market relevance or investor patience. These stories help stakeholders understand the trade-offs and strategic implications of each scheduling option.

Use storytelling to explore different scenarios (make or buy) and their potential impacts on project outcomes: Stories can effectively illustrate the consequences of decisions to either make components in-house or buy them from external suppliers. One narrative might explore the success of a project that chose to buy a key component, leading to faster project completion and reduced initial costs. Another story could examine the repercussions of manufacturing a component in-house, potentially leading to higher quality control and long-term savings but requiring upfront investment in skills and technology. Through these stories, the implications of each approach become vivid and tangible, aiding in more informed decision-making.

Create character-driven stories to highlight the roles and responsibilities of key project team members: By centering narratives around specific characters, such as a project manager or a chief engineer, these stories can highlight critical roles and responsibilities within the team. A character-driven story might follow a project manager as they navigate through complex stakeholder negotiations or how an engineer solves a critical technical problem under pressure. These stories not only demonstrate the importance of each role but also foster a deeper understanding and appreciation of team dynamics and individual contributions.

Develop narratives that describe potential risks and their impact through hypothetical scenarios: Storytelling can vividly convey potential risks and their impacts. For example, a narrative might depict a project facing a sudden supply chain disruption and how the team mitigates this risk by finding alternative suppliers or adapting project specifications. Alternatively, a story could illustrate the fallout from ignoring a known risk, such as a technical flaw, and the subsequent effect on project cost and timeline. These stories serve as cautionary tales, emphasizing the importance of risk assessment and proactive management.

By embedding these storytelling techniques into the project planning process, teams can achieve a more dynamic and effective approach to navigating complex decisions, anticipating challenges, and aligning on project goals.

How to tailor or create your own story

Insightful points	Your story
Suppose that you are on the agile context and you would like to apply waterfall on one part of the project or vis versa. You could craft a story about your success	•
Reflect on a profound experience that taught you (or someone you know) a valuable lesson about how to engage stakeholders during planning process.	•
Describe and amplify how actions and decisions were made during that experience, before and after.	•
Construct a story based on the points above	•
Share it with someone to give you feedback.	•

Takeaways

- Develop narratives that improve decision making
- Use storytelling to explore different scheduling scenarios and their potential impacts on project outcomes
- Use storytelling to explore different scenarios (make or buy) and their potential impacts on project outcomes
- Create character-driven stories to highlight the roles and responsibilities of key project team members
- Develop narratives that describe potential risks and their impact through hypothetical scenarios

The points specified above are proposed axes according to our experiences and exchange with several project managers who have experienced challenges and storytelling has helped them. As all we know, every project has its own challenges, so you could focus on a specific problem and build your own story. Stories described in this book could be used as inspiration material.

You could also combine all or part of the points above to craft your own story and adapt it to your project and stakeholders.

How to improve your story and deepen its impact

Anecdotes are powerful storytelling tools because they allow the narrator to connect with the audience on a personal level. By sharing real-life stories, storytellers humanize their message, making abstract concepts tangible and relatable. An anecdote serves as a practical example of a larger point, illustrating complex ideas in a straightforward and often entertaining manner. This method is especially useful in presentations, lectures, or even during casual conversations where capturing and maintaining the audience's interest is crucial.

Reflection, on the other hand, deepens the impact of storytelling by inviting the audience to think critically about the narrative. When a storyteller pauses to reflect, they are essentially modeling the thought process behind the insights shared. This not only builds credibility but also encourages the audience to engage with the material on a deeper level. Reflective storytelling often involves asking rhetorical questions, pondering the implications of the story, or drawing lessons from the experiences shared. This technique helps solidify the connection between the anecdote and the audience's personal experiences or challenges.

When anecdotes and reflection are combined, they create a dynamic storytelling experience that resonates deeply with listeners.

Introduction of a relatable anecdote: The story starts with a compelling, personal anecdote that introduces the main theme or problem.

Engaging through emotion: The anecdote is chosen for its emotional impact, ensuring that it captures the audience's empathy or curiosity, making the narrative more gripping.

Transition to reflection: After presenting the anecdote, the storyteller transitions into a reflective mode, discussing the lessons learned or the broader implications of the anecdote.

Invitation for audience reflection: The storyteller then invites the audience to reflect on their own experiences and how the anecdote might apply to their lives. This not only personalizes the story but also enhances its relevance.

Conclusion with a call to action: The narrative wraps up by encouraging the audience to take specific actions or to view their situations through the lens provided by the story.

By weaving together anecdotes and reflective thinking, a storyteller crafts a narrative that is both engaging and instructive, leaving a lasting impact on the audience. This approach not only makes the story more memorable but also facilitates a deeper understanding and appreciation of the message conveyed.

VIII.   Project Executing

Story: The Diamond Facet Approach

Taha, a young project manager, overflowed with enthusiasm and perseverance but sorely lacked the experience to lead complex projects. He was entrusted with the complete digitalization of the organization, a significant initiative aimed at automating processes, digitizing all relevant data, and designing dashboards to optimize decision-making. This project involved numerous stakeholders: heads of internal units, external suppliers, and regulatory authorities. His fervent commitment to the project's success caused friction with nearly all parties involved.

During a meeting meant to present the progress of the work, discussions dragged on. What was supposed to be a one-hour session stretched throughout the morning, leaving a gloomy atmosphere among the participants. Speakers followed one another, redundant, each seemingly echoing the other. Faith in the project's success crumbled, giving way to an atmosphere of reluctance and sometimes mistrust. Delays piled up.

Expectations and commitments, presented at the kick-off to the CEO, stretched far beyond projections. The needs definition phase, supposed to last a maximum of three months, bogged down into six, with endless complications. Some suppliers considered withdrawing, jeopardizing the project's future. The CEO then decided to replace Taha with Fouad, a seasoned project manager, while keeping Taha as an assistant to ensure continuity and provide him an opportunity to improve.

Fouad observed that Taha, due to his lack of experience or overly accommodating personality, tried to please all stakeholders – a venture doomed to fail. What he managed to do was nearly make them all dissatisfied. Drawing on his experience, Fouad then applied his maxim: facing stakeholders, the project manager should present himself as a facet of a diamond. Each should see a brilliance in him while sensing his unbreakable resilience. He had to highlight the future outcomes of the project while remaining firm in defending its execution. He did not hesitate to adopt various perspectives to reflect the anticipated results of the project to the concerned party, much like a facet of a diamond.

Under Fouad's leadership, the project gradually got back on track. The commitments, though challenging, were ultimately honored. The General Director asked Fouad to formalize his diamond facet approach and pass it on to young project managers, hoping to extend it to all future projects.

Now, consider your own success in comparison to using the diamond facet approach, and review your less successful experiences to see how far you have deviated from this method.

How to use storytelling during project execution process

"Facing stakeholders, the project manager should present himself as a facet of a diamond. Each should see a brilliance in him while sensing his unbreakable resilience. He had to highlight the future outcomes of the project while remaining firm in defending its execution."

Every stakeholder carries within him/her a unique spark—an inner brilliance that, if welcomed, can illuminate the entire project. But for that to happen, they must be given the space, the trust, and the right moment to bring forth what they hold most valuable. That moment is often during execution—when actions take the place of intentions, and influence shifts from theory to tangible impact. It is in this phase that true contributions emerge and hidden strengths come to light.

But all of this hinges on a single lever: the vision of the manager. The more they embrace what we previously called the diamond mindset—that rare ability to see beyond assigned roles, to recognize flashes of brilliance where others see only blind spots—the more doors they open.

Doors to engagement. Doors to collective excellence. Doors to a shared creation that transcends individual functions. Because no project shines on its own. It radiates only when each person brings their very best—and when that best is seen, welcomed, and transformed into a shared impact.

When focusing specifically on the management of project execution, storytelling becomes an invaluable tool to navigate the day-to-day operational aspects and ensure the project remains on track. Here's how storytelling can be effectively applied to the specific context of project execution:

- Develop narratives that enhance decision-making.
- Use stories to highlight achievements and milestones.
- Tell stories that focus on individual or team contributions which significantly positively impacted the project.
- When faced with a challenge, share a relevant story about a similar obstacle and how it was overcome.
- As changes occur, share stories from past projects where change led to improvement.

Fig 8 Using storytelling during Execution processes

Below Is a detailed description on how to use storytelling during execution processes.

Develop narratives that enhance decision-making during critical execution phases: During the execution phase, decisions often need to be made quickly and under pressure. Storytelling can be used to recall specific instances where swift decision-making led to overcoming imminent challenges or seizing fleeting opportunities. For example, sharing a story about how a last-minute vendor change resulted in cost savings and better resource quality can help stakeholders understand the importance of flexibility and prompt decision-making in the execution phase.

Use stories to highlight achievements and milestones specific to project execution: It's crucial to communicate the completion of specific execution milestones that are critical to the project's timeline and quality standards. For instance, a project manager might share a story about how the team managed to complete a critical phase of the project ahead of schedule despite numerous obstacles, highlighting the innovative techniques or teamwork that made this possible. This reinforces the value of the methodologies applied and encourages the team to maintain high standards of work.

Tell stories that focus on individual or team contributions to overcoming execution challenges: Recognize and share examples of team members who devised solutions to unexpected problems during the execution phase. A story could involve a technician who identified a potential fault in the equipment that could have caused significant delays and how their proactive approach saved the day. Such stories not only give credit where it's due but also set a precedent for proactive behavior and problem-solving attitude during project execution.

When faced with a challenge during execution, share a relevant story about a similar obstacle and how it was overcome: This is particularly useful in project execution when teams encounter technical or logistical challenges that seem insurmountable. By sharing a detailed story about how a previous project team navigated a similar issue — perhaps through creative workaround or an innovative application of technology — project managers can provide a blueprint for action and inspire confidence among current team members.

As changes occur during execution, share stories from past projects where change led to improvement: Project execution often involves adjustments to plans or strategies due to unforeseen circumstances or better insights. By narrating instances from past projects where adaptive changes resulted in enhanced performance or efficiency, project managers can help stakeholders and team members view changes more positively. For example, discussing how a change in the supply chain strategy reduced costs and expedited the project in the past will help in gaining buy-in for similar adjustments in the current project.

By applying storytelling specifically to these aspects of project execution, managers can ensure that their teams are not just informed but are also emotionally and intellectually engaged, helping them navigate through the complexities of project execution with greater ease and commitment.

How to adapt and create your own story

Insightful points	Your story
Think about an achievement that you realized and respect milestones	•
Think about a key team member that did a great achievement	•
Think about an approved change that was carried out successfully and has a great impact on the project	•
Reflect on one of the experiences above. What were the hows and whys that led to the success.	•
Describe and amplify how actions and decisions were made during that experience, before and after.	•
What were the lesson learned about how to engage stakeholders during planning process.	•
Construct a story based on the points above	•
Share it with someone to give you feedback.	•

Takeaways

- Develop narratives that enhance decision-making.

- Use stories to highlight achievements and milestones.

- Tell stories that focus on individual or team contributions which significantly positively impacted the project.

- When faced with a challenge, share a relevant story about a similar obstacle and how it was overcome.

- As changes occur, share stories from past projects where change led to improvement.

The points specified above are proposed axes according to our experiences and exchange with several project managers who have experienced challenges and storytelling has helped them. As all we know, every project has its own challenges, so you could focus on a specific problem and build your own story. Stories described in this book could be used as inspiration material.

You could also combine all or part of the points above to craft your own story and adapt it to your project and stakeholders.

Improve your storytelling by using the language beauty.

Remember that the story is never finished, you could improve it at any time. improving storytelling can significantly enhance how a message resonates with its audience. Two effective ways to achieve this are by using concise language and incorporating a sense of musicality into the language. Here's a deeper look at these approaches:

Using Concise Language: The power of conciseness in storytelling cannot be overstated. It involves stripping away unnecessary details to focus on the essence of the message, making the story more impactful and easier to understand. This approach respects the listener's time and attention span, which is particularly important in professional settings where time is often limited. For instance, when a project manager narrates a story about overcoming a project hurdle, focusing on the key actions, decisions, and results rather than all the preliminary discussions helps the audience grasp the critical elements of the story quickly and clearly. This clarity ensures that the core message is not lost in a sea of details, making the moral or lesson of the story stand out more distinctly.

Using Language That Has Musicality: Incorporating musicality into storytelling involves using elements like rhythm, pace, tone, and pitch variations to make the narrative more engaging. This does not mean turning the story into a song but rather being mindful of how the story sounds when spoken. A well-paced rhythm can help maintain an audience's interest and build anticipation. For example, varying the pace to slow down during a critical moment of the story can create emphasis, while speeding up during a less critical narrative can maintain energy. Additionally, the intentional use of pauses can give listeners a moment to absorb important points, similar to a rest in music that punctuates key moments. This technique makes the delivery more dynamic and can evoke stronger emotional responses from the audience.

By mastering concise language and musicality, storytellers can create compelling narratives that are not only informative but also memorable and engaging. These techniques help ensure that the story effectively conveys its message and keeps the audience engaged from beginning to end.

X.   Project Controlling and Monitoring

Story: How decision-making can go without saying

From his early days as a project manager, Taoufiq underwent a formative experience that would deeply influence his career as a manager. Here is his story.

He was tasked with managing a contract for a positioning study of an institution, before the advent of Agile methodologies. The project he led required delivering results at the end of each quarter, which had to be validated by the client. With remote collaboration tools not yet widespread, his team had to make presentations in person. Among the requirements, his counterpart had to get some deliverables approved by a lawyer. Often, the first version of the documents was delayed over minor details, such as the placement of a comma. The contract terms were unforgiving: any delay was the responsibility of the provider and resulted in penalties.

The time spent on the initial deliverables was so consuming that it threatened the total time allocated to the project. This initial failure negatively impacted the image of the organization to which Taoufiq belonged. However, he did not let this misadventure pass without learning a valuable lesson. He realized that the more he communicated regularly and openly with every stakeholder, including his team, the clearer the decisions became. He then adopted the principle of transparency and timely communication with all involved parties. Continuing his reflection, he anticipated major decisions by breaking them down into a series of logical and gradual steps. Even with project management technologies, he favored direct and sometimes informal exchanges to maintain a common dynamic. When the time came to make decisions, everything then seemed natural and evident.

Strengthened by this experience, he systematically integrated this approach into all subsequent projects, which he led successfully. Upon becoming a project director, he formalized his method under the name "natural decision-making." In his dialogues with his collaborators, he explained how nature, through minimal but constant adjustments, managed to create wonders. Emulating this process, he suggested, could radically transform our approach to decision-making.

In your own context, have you considered adopting a similar approach? Do you think it could enrich your project management strategy?

How to use storytelling during Monitoring and Controlling process

"He realized that the more he communicated regularly and openly with every stakeholder, including his team, the clearer the decisions became."

To engage is not merely to persuade. It is to bring the stakeholder back to the heart of the project's sacred fire. It is to invite them — through the clarity of the narrative and the power of meaning — to take a step, not in their own interest alone, but in service of a shared endeavor.

But that step is never taken by chance. It emerges from a climate. A space where context is not imposed, but woven. Where the conditions for success are not stated once, but reaffirmed continuously — with that quiet consistency that builds trust. A framework where transparency is not a slogan, but a mirror. Where credibility is not declared, but crafted — gesture by gesture, word by word. In such a climate, the right decision becomes natural — almost inevitable. It doesn't arise from pressure, but from clarity. And that is the subtle art of true leadership: to build an ecosystem where control does not constrain, but reveals;

where monitoring does not burden, but illuminates; where every decision, far from being a struggle, becomes an organic response to what truly makes sense.

During the monitoring and controlling phases of project management, storytelling can play a crucial role in engaging stakeholders and enhancing project success. Here's how storytelling can be effectively utilized in this context:

- Develop narratives that improve decision making
- Stories that highlight project progress, challenges faced, and solutions implemented
- Whenever a significant change is proposed, use storytelling to show how this change will affect the project and its stakeholders
- Stories to demonstrate the potential impacts of the main decisions on the project and its stakeholders. Below are some detailed descriptions on how we could use storytelling during Controling&Monitoring Processes.

Fig.9 How to use storytelling during the Controling&Monitoring processes

Develop narratives that improve decision making: Stories can be crafted to present complex decisions in a more relatable and comprehensible manner. By weaving a narrative that outlines the reasoning behind strategic decisions, the consequences of previous choices, and the anticipated outcomes of new decisions, stakeholders can gain a clearer understanding and feel more connected to the decision-making process. For example, a narrative might detail how adjusting the project scope in the past led to better resource allocation, setting a precedent for current decisions about scope adjustments.

Stories that highlight project progress, challenges faced, and solutions implemented: Regular updates on project status can be transformed into engaging stories that narrate the journey of the project. These stories can highlight key milestones reached, describe the challenges encountered along the way, and explain the solutions that were implemented. Such narratives not only keep stakeholders informed but also help maintain their interest and support by demonstrating ongoing commitment to overcoming obstacles and achieving project goals.

Whenever a significant change is proposed, use storytelling to show how this change will affect the project and its stakeholders: Introducing significant changes can often meet resistance. Storytelling can ease this process by illustrating the need for change through hypothetical or real scenarios that predict the future state of the project with and without the change. For instance, a story could depict a scenario where failing to adopt new technology results in delays and cost overruns, whereas embracing it leads to efficiency gains. This helps stakeholders visualize the practical implications of changes and aids in garnering support.

Stories to demonstrate the potential impacts of the main decisions on the project and its stakeholders: Critical decisions can have far-reaching effects on a project and its stakeholders. Creating narratives that explore these impacts can help stakeholders understand and embrace these decisions. For example, a story could be told from the perspective of various stakeholders—like a team member who benefits from a new tool, a customer who experiences improved service, or an investor concerned with cost overruns. These stories articulate the direct and indirect consequences of decisions, promoting a deeper engagement from all parties involved.

By incorporating storytelling into the monitoring and controlling processes of project management, managers can enhance stakeholder engagement, clarify complex situations, and lead projects more effectively towards their successful completion.

How to adapt and create your own story

Insightful points	Your story
Think about an important decision was made easily and quickly	•
Think about significant change was made, approved and implemented easily.	•
Think about significant challenge was faced, decision was made correctly and all stakeholders were satisfied	•
Reflect on one of the experiences above. What were the hows and whys that led to the success.	•
Describe and amplify how actions and decisions were made during that experience, before and after.	•
What were the lesson learned about how to engage stakeholders during planning process.	•
Construct a story based on the points above	•
Share it with someone to give you feedback.	•

Takeaways

- Develop narratives that improve decision making

- Develop stories that highlight project progress, challenges faced, and solutions implemented

- Whenever a significant change is proposed, use storytelling to show how this change will affect the project and its stakeholders

- Develop stories to demonstrate the potential impacts of the main decisions on the project and its stakeholders

- By making "big decision" an accumulation of small decisions, decision making will be easy and you will not be surprised that all decisions will be made without saying. The project performance will be greatly improved.

How to improve your story: Incorporate surprise

Integrating the element of surprise in storytelling, especially within the context of project management, offers several distinct advantages that can enhance communication and stakeholder engagement significantly. Here are some more nuanced ways to effectively leverage this storytelling element:

Highlighting Adaptability and Innovation: When unexpected events are woven into the narrative, they naturally highlight the team's ability to adapt and innovate. For example, if a story recounts how a project team faced a sudden regulatory change that threatened to derail their schedule, the narrative could then reveal an innovative solution or workaround that the team developed. This not only surprises the listener but also reinforces the message that the team is skilled, resourceful, and capable of turning potential disasters into opportunities.

Enhancing Learning Outcomes: Surprise elements in stories can enhance learning by making lessons more memorable. When project stakeholders hear about unexpected problems and the creative solutions employed to solve them, these scenarios are likely to stick with them longer than straightforward, predictable narratives. This method of storytelling can be particularly effective in training sessions or workshops, where real-life tales of unexpected challenges and resolutions can serve as practical learning tools for project management professionals.

Building Narrative Tension: In any story, building tension is crucial to keeping the audience engaged. In the realm of project management, introducing a sudden twist — such as an unforeseen technological failure or a critical stakeholder withdrawing support — can create a narrative tension that compels the audience to stay tuned for the resolution. This tension, followed by a satisfying resolution, not only makes the story more engaging but also mimics the real-life highs and lows of managing a project, providing a relatable and instructive experience for stakeholders.

Fostering Emotional Connection: Surprises can evoke a wide range of emotions, from shock and worry to relief and joy. By incorporating these emotional elements into project updates or presentations, the storyteller can create a stronger emotional connection with the audience. For instance, sharing a surprising success story — such as an underperforming project area that turned around dramatically due to a team member's unexpected insight—can inspire and uplift the audience, strengthening their emotional investment in the project's outcome.

Encouraging Engagement and Discussion: Surprising elements in a narrative can spark discussions and encourage deeper engagement from stakeholders. After presenting a story with a surprising element, a project manager might ask the audience how they would have handled the situation, what they can learn from it, or how it might apply to other project areas. This approach not only makes meetings more interactive but also helps to foster a culture of openness and collaborative problem-solving.

Incorporating the element of surprise in storytelling within project management is not just about keeping the audience entertained; it's a strategic tool that can enhance understanding, learning, and engagement, ultimately contributing to more successful project outcomes and stronger team dynamics.

XI.   Project Closing

Story: finishing with mastery

Karim was leading a significant project on modeling and optimizing organizational processes, under the watchful eye of the executive management. For him, the challenge lay not only in the success of the project but also in his ability to close it on time, leveraging the power of the executive leadership. Hicham, who headed one of the units, saw this influence as an encroachment on his domain of responsibility. Once the project was closed and the documents were shared, including with Hicham's unit, it exacerbated his growing reluctance. He seized every opportunity to criticize the system, jeopardizing the collaboration within projects led by Karim.

The situation worsened; each project under Karim's stewardship suffered from Hicham's team's resistance, making collaboration arduous. Influenced by this dynamic, other entities also expressed their dissatisfaction. In hindsight, Karim recognized that taking more time to ease tensions and satisfy Hicham might have been beneficial.

During a conversation with a musician friend, the latter revealed that excellence in music does not lie so much in the ability to play a piece with professionalism, but rather in finishing it with mastery. Karim then drew a parallel between project management and the art of musical performance. Just like in literature or cinema, the ending of a work can defines its success in the eyes of the audience.

From then on, Karim resolved not to close any project or phase without the full agreement of key stakeholders. He saw closure as a preparation for the post-project phase, seeking to ensure a good appropriation of the outcomes. He even considered adding a dedicated phase for the adoption of the solutions provided, to close each project with excellence and leave no lingering issues, even in the minds of stakeholders. For him, project management became an art, at the crossroads of various disciplines, deserving to be treated as such.

Have you ever faced similar situations? How did you manage to resolve them? Do Karim's experiences inspire you?

How to use storytelling during project Closing

"Karim then drew a parallel between project management and the art of musical performance. Just like in literature or cinema, the ending of a work can defines its success in the eyes of the audience."

Closing a project should never be seen as the end of a chapter, but rather as the opening of a new door. Closure is not an ending—it's a transition. A subtle threshold leading to a future still in the making, a dormant potential waiting to unfold—elsewhere, differently, tomorrow. Embracing this mindset means seeing differently. It means recognizing, behind every signed-off deliverable and every formal approval, more than just a satisfied client or a punctual supplier. It means seeing a partner—a contributor to the present, and perhaps to what's yet to come. Because true project intelligence doesn't stop at managing the now. It's rooted in a forward-facing posture, in the ability to preserve, to nurture, to extend relationships beyond the formal end. Offering attention not because an immediate need demands it, but because a shared future can still be imagined.

Storytelling is a uniquely powerful tool in project management, especially during the closing phase. As projects wrap up, it's crucial to reflect on the journey, celebrate successes, and consolidate lessons learned. Employing storytelling techniques can enhance this process by making it more engaging and memorable for all involved. By articulating key successes and milestones, conducting workshops for sharing insights, explaining the relevance of deliverables, and sharing personal journeys, storytelling transforms standard project closures into profound learning and celebratory experiences. This approach not only encapsulates the essence of the project's achievements but also reinforces team solidarity and paves the way for future successes. Below are the main points where you could use storytelling during project closing.

- Use storytelling to underscore key successes and milestones reached during the project.
- Conduct storytelling workshops where team members can share stories about lessons learned.
- Utilize storytelling to clarify the context of deliverables and their potential applications.

- Organize a closing meeting where team members can share personal stories from their project journey.
- Craft a narrative to share at a celebratory closing event that captures the essence of the project's journey.

Let's dive in how to use storytelling during Closing Processes.

Fig.10.Storytelling and Closing Processes

Use storytelling to underscore key successes and milestones reached during the project. Storytelling can be a powerful tool to highlight the significant achievements and milestones of a project. By crafting compelling narratives around each success, you provide a memorable and engaging way for team members and stakeholders to appreciate the impact of their efforts. This approach not only celebrates progress but also reinforces the value of the work completed, encouraging a sense of accomplishment and pride among the team.

Conduct storytelling workshops where team members can share stories about lessons learned. Facilitate storytelling workshops to create a platform for team members to exchange insights and experiences gained throughout the project. These sessions allow participants to reflect on challenges faced, solutions devised, and personal growth experienced. Sharing these stories fosters a culture of learning and continuous improvement, helping team members apply these lessons to future projects and enhancing team cohesion through shared experiences.

Utilize storytelling to clarify the context of deliverables and their potential applications. Storytelling can effectively convey the broader context and potential uses of project deliverables. By telling the story of how these outputs were developed and envisioning their impact, you can help stakeholders understand their significance and practical applications. This method ensures that deliverables are seen not just as end products but as vital components of a larger narrative, enhancing their perceived value and utility.

Organize a closing meeting where team members can share personal stories from their project journey. At the project's conclusion, organize a meeting dedicated to sharing personal stories from the journey. This gathering serves as an intimate forum for team members to express their experiences, challenges, triumphs, and transformations. Sharing these personal narratives helps to humanize the project process, strengthen bonds between team members, and provide closure to the collective endeavor.

Craft a narrative to share at a celebratory closing event that captures the essence of the project's journey. Develop a cohesive and engaging narrative to be shared at a celebratory closing event, encapsulating the entire project journey. This narrative should highlight the project's inception, critical milestones, obstacles overcome, and the ultimate outcomes. By presenting this story, you celebrate the collective effort and dedication of the team, offering a sense of closure and achievement. It serves not only as a record of what was accomplished but also as a source of inspiration for future initiatives.

How to adapt and create your own story

Insightful points	Your story
Think about an important decision was made easily and quickly	•
Think about significant key successes and milestones reached during the project.	•
Think deeply about the context of better using deliverables and their potential applications	•
Think about a great success of a team or team member to capitalize on it	•
Reflect on one of the experiences above. What were the hows and whys that led to the success.	•
Describe and amplify how actions and decisions were made during that experience, before and after.	•
What were the lesson learned about how to engage stakeholders during closing process.	•
Construct a story based on the points above	•
Share it with someone to give you feedback.	•

Takeaways

- Use storytelling to underscore key successes and milestones reached during the project.

- Conduct storytelling workshops where team members can share stories about lessons learned.

- Utilize storytelling to clarify the context of deliverables and their potential applications.

- Organize a closing meeting where team members can share personal stories from their project journey.

- Craft a narrative to share at a celebratory closing event that captures the essence of the project's journey.

- Remember that project management is the excellence does not lie so much in the ability to play a piece with professionalism, but rather in finishing it with mastery.

- Project management becomes an art, at the crossroads of various disciplines, deserving to be treated as such.

How to improve your storytelling? Amplify emotion

Amplifying emotions is a pivotal technique in refining storytelling, especially in the context of project management and team collaboration. Emotions are the heartbeat of a story; they transform basic narratives into compelling, relatable, and memorable experiences. By heightening emotional elements, storytellers can forge a deeper connection with their audience, making the message not only heard but also felt.

When it comes to project management, amplifying emotions can significantly enhance the impact of the story being told. For instance, sharing the challenges and triumphs of a project can evoke feelings of suspense and joy, respectively. This emotional engagement helps team members and stakeholders to experience the highs and lows of the project journey as if they were their own. It creates a more profound appreciation for the work done and the hurdles overcome, fostering a deeper sense of belonging and achievement among all involved.

Moreover, emotional amplification allows the audience to internalize lessons learned more effectively. For example, discussing a major setback in a project with genuine emotional insight into the team's frustration and eventual resolution makes the lesson stickier. Listeners are more likely to remember and learn from these emotional highs and lows, which can guide future decision-making and improve resilience.

Furthermore, using emotions strategically can also highlight the human aspect of project work, promoting empathy and support within the team. When team members openly share their personal feelings about various phases of the project, it encourages others to express their emotions and vulnerabilities, which can lead to stronger, more supportive team dynamics.

Overall, amplifying emotions in storytelling within project closures not only captivates the audience but also enhances the educational and communal value of the narratives shared. It makes the closure not just a procedural formality but a meaningful and impactful conclusion to the project's journey.

PART III: HOW TO TAILOR STORYTELLING TO TYPES OF STAKEHOLDERS

XII. How to engage specific stakeholders

Story: Weave bonds based on mutual trust, almost brotherly

Abdou, still in the early stages of his career as a chief engineer, was entrusted by the director of his entity with a delicate mission: to resolve a conflict between two departments of the organization concerning the management of a supply contract. The case, thorny and stagnant, was caught between the user entity and the supply management entity. Fortunately, Abdou maintained harmonious relationships and a certain affinity with the heads of these two entities.

This was no minor contract; the supplier was even threatening to start legal proceedings against the organization. Many predicted Abdou's failure due to his lack of experience. However, this file was just one among many mired in internal conflict.

As tensions escalated, Abdou came close to giving up. Each attempt to discuss the issue with one of the heads resulted in a flood of harsh criticisms against the other side, described as incompetent and malicious, excelling only at "throwing stones in the other's path," to use their own words. Curiously, the accusations from each side mirrored each other with remarkable similarity.

In a last-ditch effort, driven by the fear of failure but also by a steadfast will, Abdou decided to meet separately with the protagonists over coffee. During these exchanges, he merely sought clarifications and interspersed the conversation with light anecdotes to relax the atmosphere.

To his great surprise, he discovered that the demands of each party were merely distorted echoes of the other's statements. Armed with this revelation, he crafted a resolution proposal that was quickly adopted by both parties.

From this experience, Abdou learned a valuable lesson: before requesting anything from a stakeholder, before engaging them or entrusting them with a mission, it is crucial to establish a friendly, almost complicit rapport. Since then, in every project he was involved in, he strove to gain access to key stakeholders and weave bonds based on mutual trust, almost brotherly. His increasingly evident success attested to the effectiveness of his approach.

Have you ever faced similar situations to that of Abdou? What approach did you adopt to navigate through these challenges?

Background to engage specific stakeholders

"…before requesting anything from a stakeholder, before engaging them or entrusting them with a mission, it is crucial to establish a friendly, almost complicit rapport. Since then, in every project he was involved in, he strove to gain access to key stakeholders and weave bonds based on mutual trust, almost brotherly. His increasingly evident success attested to the effectiveness of his approach." This is a great lesson from the above story.

When it comes to engaging specific stakeholders, simply conveying information is not enough. First, you must build a connection. Not just a point of contact, but a living relationship, woven from mutual respect — and at times, from the unspoken understanding of a shared vision.

True influence is born from rooted relationships. Not forced. Not faked. A relationship that allows itself to grow, to explore different layers of exchange — from the glance that acknowledges, to the words that confide. And this is where storytelling becomes a lever. Not to charm, but to build. Not to persuade, but to bring forth a shared truth. More than a tool, storytelling becomes a bridge. It's not just about speaking — it's about connecting. And once that connection is made, only then can the narrative serve deeper purposes: strategy, mobilization, transformation. But without relationship, there is no story that resonates. And without story, no relationship that endures.

In a world where projects are increasingly complex and expansive, touching multiple domains, stakeholder management has become a more sophisticated and essential exercise. Modern projects do not just mark out known territories; they navigate through mosaics of interests and often changing influences, making the art of stakeholder management a delicate and strategic dance.

Fig. 11:Engage specific stakeholders

Today's stakeholders are numerous, and their interactions complex, often interdependent. This web of mutual influences sketches a landscape where each stakeholder may be involved in several aspects of a project. Their power and influence, far from static, evolve with the project, thus altering the tableau of their commitments and needs. This reality complicates the traditional mapping of stakeholders, which typically categorizes them into four quadrants [1]: those with high influence and high interest, those with high influence but low interest, those with low influence but high interest, and finally, those with low influence and low interest.

These quadrants, far from isolated, function more like communicating vessels, where the waters of power and interest flow freely, modifying levels and dynamics continuously. This fluidity demands constant adaptation of management strategies, requiring project managers to be more vigilant and flexible.

The crucial question then becomes: how can we rely on the four basic strategies to develop a holistic and adaptive approach that accounts for the variable portion of the four quadrants for each stakeholder? The answer lies in a tailored strategy, a symphony where each note is played in harmony with the project's evolution.

Firstly, it is essential to develop a deep understanding of the project's ecosystem. This involves identifying not only who the stakeholders are but also how their levels of influence and interest evolve throughout the project. The use of dynamic tracking tools can help visualize these changes and adjust strategies accordingly.

Secondly, communication must be modulated based on the evolution of these parameters. For stakeholders with high influence, whether interested or not, regular and targeted briefings are crucial. This ensures they remain informed and ready to intervene if necessary. Concurrently, for those with high interest, mechanisms for feedback and sessions of active engagement can maintain their support and value their contributions.

Thirdly, the flexibility of engagement plans must allow for the incorporation of new stakeholders or the repositioning of existing ones into new quadrants. Periodic reviews of stakeholder management strategies and proactive adjustments are essential to stay aligned with project objectives while respecting changing dynamics.

Finally, fostering a culture of recognition and mutual respect among all stakeholders can help balance powers and interests over time. This creates an environment where even the least influential parties feel that their voice counts, thus enhancing their potential engagement. Adopting an integrated and evolving strategy in stakeholder management is not merely an option but a necessity in the context of contemporary projects. Like a conductor, the project manager must know when and how to play each note of the different strategies to maintain the project's symphony in perfect harmony.

To effectively adopt a customized strategy for engaging a specific stakeholder, it is critically important to first establish and maintain rapport with them, or to build a pathway for access. This foundational step is crucial because it sets the stage for all subsequent interactions and determines the depth and quality of the relationship. Building rapport with a stakeholder involves understanding their needs, preferences, and communication styles. This can be achieved through attentive listening, showing genuine interest in their concerns, and empathizing with their position. When stakeholders feel understood and valued, they are more likely to be cooperative and open in their communications, which facilitates smoother and more effective project management.

Maintaining rapport requires consistent effort. Regular updates, timely responses to inquiries, and ongoing check-ins are all part of this process. It's also important to demonstrate reliability by following through on commitments and showing respect for the stakeholder's time and contributions. This consistency builds trust, a critical element in any business relationship.

Constructing access to a stakeholder might involve more strategic approaches, especially if initial contact is challenging due to the stakeholder's position or schedule constraints. This might include leveraging mutual connections for introductions, attending the same professional events, or participating in forums and discussions that attract their interest. Once access is gained, it's vital to maximize the opportunity by establishing credibility. This can be done by sharing insights, providing value through information or resources, and aligning your discussions with their strategic interests.

In sum, the initial steps of building and maintaining rapport, along with constructing access to stakeholders, are not merely preliminary actions but are integral to developing a tailored engagement strategy. These efforts ensure that communication lines are open and productive, paving the way for a cooperative relationship that can significantly influence the success of a project.

Story: Engaging with beauty

Dokou served as the principal client in a project orchestrated by my friend Nasser. Nasser was part of an organization dedicated to implementing societal actions wherever it operated. Dokou, responsible for territorial development at an institution in a Saharan African country, operated in an environment where powerful and influential NGOs and equally significant political opposition played a crucial role. Senior executives, to position themselves, would align with political parties and forge connections with certain associations.

Nasser and his team had meticulously prepared all the required deliverables. Following their presentation, although Dokou's team raised no criticisms and seemed satisfied, the deliverables remained unvalidated. One day, a member of the recipient team confided in Nasser that the institution's leaders wanted a specific societal action, similar to those carried out elsewhere by the organization, to benefit the local BAMBA association. However, Nasser had already provided the association with a potable water well, unbeknownst to Dokou. Nasser quickly worked to inform him. Nonetheless, it was essential that this information did not leak and that the initiative appeared spontaneous.

This experience taught Nasser that it was not enough to merely meet the direct expectations of the team representing the client. It was crucial to also inform the client about actions taken with other potentially influential stakeholders, closely monitor any information dissemination that could be used to manipulate the actors involved, and ensure a thorough follow-up of each key stakeholder to monitor their influence.

From then on, Nasser viewed stakeholder engagement as a symphony where each strategy and action harmoniously integrates to either positively influence or counteract negative influences. This model, akin to a natural arrangement, not only engages but delights with its beauty.

I invite you to take a moment to reflect on the successes you have achieved in stakeholder engagement. Compare your approach to Nasser's, identify possible improvements, and consider strategies to implement them in the future.

Assessing Influence Dynamics

Mapping stakeholders is essential — but it's only the first breath. Because today, what truly matters is not just who is present... but how each one influences the other. It's that invisible web — a network of tensions, alliances, silences, and echoes — that we must learn to read. A living map.

Engaging a stakeholder is never an isolated act. It means stepping into a dynamic flow. It's setting foot on shifting ground, crisscrossed by currents and channels of influence where every gesture, every word, can echo far. Very far. So, it's no longer just about speaking. It's about tuning into the vibrations. Adapting the narrative. Choosing your words the way you'd choose keys — carefully, intentionally. Because each channel calls for its own language, its own rhythm. And it's in that narrative precision that true engagement begins. In other words: understanding the links in order to weave meaning. Reading invisible forces to craft a story that brings them together.

Mapping stakeholders is a crucial step in ensuring the success of any project management initiative. By identifying who the stakeholders are, understanding their relationships, analyzing their interactions, and assessing the dynamics of influence and power among them, project managers can better engage and align these key individuals or groups with the project's objectives.

Identifying the Stakeholders: Identifying stakeholders involves pinpointing everyone who has a vested interest in the project or will be affected by its outcomes. This can include internal stakeholders such as project team members, management, and other employees, as well as external stakeholders like clients, suppliers, investors, community members, and regulatory bodies. The goal is to create a comprehensive list of individuals and groups that encompasses both direct and indirect influencers of the project.

Understanding Stakeholder Relationships: Understanding the relationships between stakeholders involves analyzing how they are connected. This may include hierarchical relationships within an organization, partnerships between enterprises, or informal networks that influence project dynamics. Recognizing these relationships helps in predicting potential alliances or conflicts. A stakeholder relationship map can be a useful tool here, visually representing the links between various parties and indicating the nature of their connections (supportive, neutral, or oppositional).

Analyzing Stakeholder Interactions: Analyzing how stakeholders interact with each other involves observing or inquiring about their communication and collaboration patterns. This includes understanding the formal channels of communication, such as scheduled meetings and official correspondences, as well as the informal interactions that might occur. Identifying these interactions helps in understanding the flow of information and decision-making processes within the stakeholder network, which is critical for managing expectations and facilitating effective engagement.

Assessing Influence Dynamics: Stakeholders often have varying degrees of power and influence, which can affect others within the project scope. Analyzing how one stakeholder can influence another involves understanding their source of power—whether it is derived from their position, expertise, control over resources, or their ability to influence public opinion. It's also important to consider how stakeholders might leverage their power to affect the project positively or negatively. Understanding these dynamics is crucial for anticipating potential risks and opportunities and for strategizing on how to best engage each stakeholder.

Every stakeholder has a base of power, which can derive from several sources:

Positional Power. Often held by high-ranking individuals such as executives or government officials, positional power comes from the authority of a role within an organization or community. Expert Power: This stems from a stakeholder's expertise and knowledge in a specific area that is critical to the project. Experts can influence decisions through their insights and experience. Resource Power: Control over critical resources — financial, human, or material — gives stakeholders the power to influence project scopes, timelines, and priorities. Network Power: Influential stakeholders may possess extensive networks and can mobilize support or opposition through their contacts. Informational Power: Stakeholders with exclusive, timely, and relevant information can wield significant influence over project decisions and outcomes.

Understanding these power sources helps in predicting how stakeholders might use their power in relation to the project. Once power sources are identified, the next step is to map how this power connects stakeholders within the project.

Influence network mapping involves: Visualizing Connections: Create diagrams to visualize the relationships between power and influence among stakeholders. This helps in identifying key influencers and understanding the flow of influence across the network. Analyzing Influence Pathways: Determine how influence flows from one stakeholder to another. For instance, a senior manager might influence middle management, who in turn influence front-line employees.

Evaluating the potential influence of stakeholders involves understanding how their power can affect the project. This includes: Support vs. Opposition: Identifying who is likely to support or oppose the project based on their interests and how they might leverage their power to influence others. Scenario Planning: Develop scenarios to anticipate how stakeholders might react to different project decisions and milestones. This can help in preparing responses and strategies to harness or mitigate their influence.

This comprehensive stakeholder mapping not only aids in initial planning but also serves as a guide throughout the project lifecycle, ensuring that all interactions and engagements are thoughtfully managed and aligned with the project's goals.

Takeaways

o First of all, build rapport. Weave bonds based on mutual trust, almost brotherly.

o Mapping stakeholders is just a first step, it is necessary to

o Understand Stakeholder Relationships:

o Assess Influence Dynamics. Stakeholders are inter-influenced

o View stakeholder engagement as a symphony where each strategy and action harmoniously integrate to either positively influence or counteract negative influences including:

  - To satisfy

  - To watch closely

  - To keep inform

Next chapters will detail how to engage each kind of stakeholders and to tailor storytelling. Besides, they will clarify how to prepare the ground for stakeholders' engagement and more importantly, how to use storytelling to make sense out of complexity.

XIII. Keep stakeholders informed

Story: How to communicate a crucial information to a highly emotional crowd

This project involved constructing a gold processing plant in an arid area where the groundwater, extremely sensitive, was vital for the survival of the local residents and their livestock.

One morning, Salim, who was leading this project, received an urgent call from the construction site manager. He was informed that the site was at a standstill: the local residents had started a protest and were planning a prolonged sit-in. They refused to negotiate; their only demand was the definitive halt of the construction. Their anger stemmed from fears that the gold extraction process, which allegedly included cyanidation according to their sources, would severely threaten the groundwater, endangering their lives and that of their animals.

Salim was aware that any delay in construction could not only jeopardize the project's success but also tarnish the company's image, which was already engaged in talks with potential long-term clients. Adding irony to the situation, Salim knew full well that the process adopted for extracting gold from the ore did not involve the use of cyanide at all. The challenge was how to communicate this crucial information to a highly emotional crowd.

He then chose to speak, not to dispute, but to share the story of a similar mine in another country, where the process included cyanidation with disastrous consequences. He also told the story of Kamel, a worker who alone supported his large family. Kamel dreamed of providing his children with quality education. However, he died prematurely, succumbed to a disease exacerbated by exposure to cyanide, leaving behind a shattered future.

In an almost sacred silence, Salim then revealed the truth: "Fortunately, our extraction method does not use cyanide, thank God." He then offered to technically train a few volunteers on the employed process, using simple and accessible terms. This initiative bore fruit: the explanations reassured the residents, and the crisis was defused. Later, in a discussion with a colleague, Salim confided: "To engage them, you must first understand them; and to understand them, it's crucial to put yourself in their shoes while keeping in mind my responsibility to successfully lead this project."

Since then, Salim's experience has been cited as a model of crisis management.

Have you ever faced a similar situation? What was your reaction? How does Salim's story inspire you?

How to keep stakeholders informed

"To engage them, you must first understand them; and to understand them, it's crucial to put yourself in their shoes while keeping in mind my responsibility to successfully lead this project." Is a great lesson from Salim Story.

Keeping someone informed is not about passing on data. It's about weaving a thread. We often mistakenly believe that informing a stakeholder means handing over facts like leaflets on a street corner. But no — it's much more than that. Truly keeping someone informed is like offering a key. And every key implies a door. The right moment. A hand ready to receive it.

Behind every act of communication lies a delicate balance between what the other person is ready to hear and what the project needs them to understand. It depends on their state — emotional, intellectual, relational. It also depends on the breath of the moment: is the information critical? Or simply helpful? But all of that is just the surface.

The real foundation, the one we often forget, is this: the project manager must always know more than the stakeholder. Not to dominate, but to guide. To discern what should be said, and what can wait. To use silence as a tool, not as a void. Before speaking, one must listen. Observe. Sense. Of course, gather the data—but more importantly, detect the subtle signals: the fears, the expectations, the triggers for engagement. Only then can the time for sharing truly come. And when that moment comes, the information must be shared as a story. Because raw data informs. But a story—a story transforms. It lights the way forward, gives meaning to uncertainty, and unites people around a future that has yet to be built.

In the context of project management, engaging stakeholders is crucial for the success of any project. Effective engagement ensures that all parties involved are informed, supportive, and active participants in the project's progression. Below, we explore why each of the following points is necessary and how they impact project success:

Fig. 11 Keep stakeholders informed

Determine the information that prevails among stakeholders. Understanding the information that stakeholders consider most important allows project managers to tailor communication strategies effectively. This ensures that all discussions are relevant and address the stakeholders' concerns and priorities. By prioritizing this information, stakeholders feel valued and understood, which fosters trust and a stronger commitment to the project. This alignment of priorities reduces conflicts and ensures smoother project execution.

Share facts with stakeholders. Sharing accurate and factual information with stakeholders keeps everyone on the same page and prevents misunderstandings that could derail the project. It establishes a foundation of transparency and accountability. This approach builds confidence in the project management process, enhancing stakeholder support and cooperation. It also ensures that decision-making is informed and based on reliable data, leading to more effective outcomes.

Distribute relevant information to stakeholders. Not all information is pertinent to every stakeholder. Tailoring the information to the needs and roles of different stakeholders ensures that they receive only what is necessary and applicable to their interests and responsibilities. Targeted communication prevents information overload and keeps stakeholders engaged without overwhelming them with irrelevant details. This relevance makes it easier for stakeholders to respond appropriately and take necessary actions, thereby accelerating project progress.

Ensure stakeholders have received the relevant information and understand it as intended. It's not enough to simply distribute information; it must also be confirmed that the information was received and correctly interpreted. This step is crucial to avoid miscommunications that can lead to costly errors or delays. Ensuring clarity and understanding prevents rework and delays, as stakeholders are more likely to perform their roles effectively when they fully grasp the information. It also reinforces trust and reliability among the project team and its stakeholders, promoting a cooperative and proactive project environment.

By adhering to these points, project managers can significantly enhance stakeholder engagement, which is directly linked to the project's overall success. Each step contributes to building a robust framework for communication, collaboration, and joint effort towards achieving project goals.

How to adapt and create your own story

+Insightful points	Your story
Think about a key stakeholder who do you have to inform.	•
Think about significant stake that will impact the project success, positively or negatively.	•
Think about the important role that has the stakeholder.	•
Think about a great success of you, a team or team member who manage this issue.	•
Reflect on what said above. What were the hows and whys that led to the success.	•
Describe and amplify how actions and decisions were made during that experience, before and after.	•
What were the lesson learned about how to best keep the stakeholders informed.	•
Construct a story based on the points above	•
Share it with someone to give you feedback.	•

Takeaways

o Determine the information that prevails among stakeholders.

o Share facts with stakeholders

o Distribute relevant information to stakeholders.

o Ensure stakeholders have received the relevant information and understand it as intended.

As Salim Said: To engage stakeholders by keeping them informed, you must first understand them; and to understand them, it's crucial to put yourself in their shoes while keeping in mind my responsibility is to successfully lead this project.

XIV.   Watch stakeholders closely

Story:the course water

In a context where parameters were constantly fluctuating – material prices, labor costs, and consumables – the contract procedure, dictated by existing laws and processes, required that all prices be indexed to the market. Hamid, who was in charge of constructing a section of the highway, coordinated with several suppliers for the construction and procurement of raw materials. Among them, Bituma was responsible for delivering asphalt, essential for road construction.

Within three months, the price of asphalt plummeted by nearly 40%, leading to an almost proportional decrease in Bituma's profit relative to its revenue. Worse still, financial forecasts had been established based on this major revenue. Bituma was forced to revise these forecasts downward, impacting its stock price. Shareholders were outraged, believing that the management had not based its strategic plan on sufficiently solid foundations. They then considered terminating the contract, or at least renegotiating it.

Hamid, closely observing the fluctuations in material prices and their impact on stakeholders, saw this drop as an opportunity to expand the scope of the project by increasing the planned number of linear kilometers. He prepared a study in this regard and submitted a request for modification, which was approved by the steering committee since it did not have a significant impact on the project's budget. He also proceeded with replanning to minimize the impact of the change on the scheduled timelines.

When the representative from Bituma came to renegotiate the contract, brandishing the threat of termination, he was surprised by the already approved modification request. Hamid could not have hoped for a better outcome and thus secured the project's advancement, as well as the trust and satisfaction of Bituma.

What's interesting is that Hamid gained the trust of Bituma Corporation, and during the COVID pandemic, they considered the projects led by Hamid and his team as a priority for their supply chain.

During a discussion with one of his colleagues about this experience, he shared his philosophy: "My inspiration is water, the source of life. Water does not settle in any determined form, nor does it stop in any particular place. It is the most alert because it constantly renews itself and adapts to the force of nature. And most importantly, it gives life to those within its reach. That is why its course never ceases to progress."

Facing geopolitical, economic, and environmental changes, you will surely encounter situations similar to what Hamid experienced. If that's already the case, how have you analyzed the trends and anticipated their impact on the project and its key stakeholders? What inspiration have you drawn from Hamid's experience?

How to watch stakeholders closely

"...Water does not settle in any determined form, nor does it stop in any particular place. It is the most alert because it constantly renews itself and adapts to the force of nature. And most importantly, it gives life to those within its reach. That is why its course never ceases to progress." To watch a stakeholder, you need to be as water: the most alert because it constantly renews itself and adapts to the force of nature.

Watching a stakeholder is like dancing with a living system. It's not just about watching. It's about perceiving. Sensing. Decoding the subtle shifts of a human ecosystem in constant motion. To watch them closely is not to spy — it's to accompany from a respectful distance, in silence, like watching over a star in the night sky. Not to influence them immediately, but to be ready. Ready to engage the moment their orbit intersects with that of the project.

And for that, you need an invisible discipline. A flexible mind. Unshakable resilience. The kind of self-mastery that weathers any storm. And above all, an art — the art of gathering information, organizing it without freezing it, and listening for the hidden music within it — that secret logic that speaks louder than words. Because in the art of following lies the art of understanding. And in the art of understanding, the wisdom to know when to speak. When to act. When to sow.In other words: to read a moving being without ever trying to make them stand still.

Watching closely how stakeholders respond and react to changes in a project or organization can significantly enhance your ability to manage change effectively and optimize effort. Here's how this can be accomplished:

Fig. 12 Watch Stakeholders

Early Identification of Concerns and Resistances. By observing stakeholders closely, you can quickly identify any concerns or resistance they might have towards the change. This early detection allows you to address issues before they become significant obstacles, ensuring a smoother transition and reducing the effort required to implement changes.

Tailored Communication. Understanding each stakeholder's interests, goals, and fears through close observation enables you to tailor your communication strategies. Personalized messaging that addresses specific concerns and highlights benefits relevant to each stakeholder can foster greater acceptance and support for the change.

Engagement and Buy-in. Closely watching stakeholders helps you determine the best ways to engage them. By involving them in the change process, soliciting their input, and making them feel valued, you increase their buy-in and commitment. This collaborative approach not only eases the change management process but also enhances the quality and sustainability of the change.

Predicting Stakeholder Behavior. By observing stakeholders' reactions to past changes or similar situations, you can predict how they might react to future changes. This predictive insight allows you to proactively plan and implement strategies that align with stakeholders' behaviors and preferences, thus optimizing the effort required for managing change.

Continuous Improvement. Ongoing observation allows you to see what works and what doesn't in real-time, enabling continuous improvement of your change management strategies. By adapting your approach based on direct feedback and observed behaviors, you can make more informed decisions and refine your methods to be more effective and less resource-intensive.

Building Trust and Relationships. Watching and responding to stakeholders' needs and concerns helps build trust and strengthen relationships. Trust is crucial in change management as it facilitates open communication, reduces uncertainties, and increases the likelihood of stakeholders supporting future changes.

Mitigating Risks. Close observation helps in identifying potential risks associated with stakeholder reactions. By foreseeing these risks, you can develop mitigation strategies in advance, thereby reducing the impact of negative outcomes and ensuring the change process remains on track. By focusing on stakeholder observations, change managers can craft a more strategic approach that minimizes resistance, maximizes engagement, and efficiently allocates resources to ensure successful change implementation.

However, As Robert Mckee said[1], every person/character live in three spheres, one inside the other.A self within a self within a self. The innermost sphere churns with the unsayable; the middle sphere restrains the unsaid; the outer sphere releases the said. In order the watch a stakeholder closely, we need to pay attention to the three spheres.

To effectively engage stakeholders, it's crucial to understand the complex layers of communication and thought that each individual harbors. These layers can be visualized as three concentric spheres: the said, the unsaid, and the unsayable. Each sphere represents different levels of communication and internal experience, influencing how stakeholders interact in any professional setting.

The outermost sphere is the "said" — the realm of explicit communication. This includes spoken words, written communications, and all forms of direct expression. At this level, stakeholders share their thoughts, feedback, decisions, and instructions. It is the most accessible layer and forms the basis of our understanding of their positions, needs, and expectations.

Importance of the Said: Paying attention to what is said is fundamental in any interaction. It provides the explicit content needed to perform tasks, make decisions, and align team efforts with organizational goals. Observing and responding to this layer helps in maintaining clear and efficient communication, ensuring that all parties are informed and that project objectives are understood and met.

Beneath the surface lies the "unsaid" — the thoughts and feelings stakeholders have chosen not to express openly. This might include reservations about a strategy, unspoken expectations, or underlying concerns about a project's direction. The unsaid can be inferred through body language, tone of voice, hesitation, and what is omitted from communication.

Importance of the Unsaid: Engaging with the unsaid is crucial for deeper stakeholder relations. It helps in anticipating potential issues before they become overt problems and aids in building trust. By paying attention to non-verbal cues and reading between the lines, one can address concerns that are not directly voiced, fostering a more collaborative and supportive environment.

The innermost sphere, the "unsayable," contains thoughts and feelings that are deeply personal or subconscious. It represents the Deepest need and desire that incite a stakeholder's choices and actions. It could be expressed under the pressure of life These may include fears, dreams, deep-seated beliefs, and core values that influence stakeholder behavior in subtle but profound ways. The unsayable is typically not disclosed due to its intimate nature or because it might be too complex to articulate.

Importance of the Unsayable: Understanding the unsayable can provide profound insights into a stakeholder's motivations and potential biases. Although it is the most challenging to access, getting a sense of this layer can lead to more empathetic and nuanced interactions. By recognizing and respecting this depth, you can engage stakeholders in a way that honors their full selves, leading to more meaningful and committed partnerships.

Paying attention to these three spheres — the said, the unsaid, and the unsayable — allows for a comprehensive understanding of stakeholders. It enables you to not only react to what is openly shared but also to anticipate needs and address deeper concerns, thereby fostering trust and collaboration. This holistic approach can significantly enhance project outcomes and stakeholder satisfaction by ensuring that all dimensions of human communication are considered and respected.

How to adapt and create your own story

Insightful points	Your story
Think about a key stakeholder whose power or influence has changed during the project course.	•
According of the change above, think about significant stake that will impact the project success, positively or negatively.	•
Think about a great success of you, a team or team member who manage this issue by positively surprising the stakeholder.	•
Reflect on what said above. What were the hows and whys that led to the success.	•
Describe and amplify how actions and decisions were made during that experience, before and after.	•
What were the lesson learned about how to watch stakeholders as a system.	•
Construct a story based on the points above	•
Share it with someone to give you feedback.	•

Takeaways

- Early Identification of Concerns and Resistances

- Understanding each stakeholder's interests, goals, and fears through close observation

- Closely watching stakeholders helps you determine the best ways to engage them.

- By observing stakeholders' reactions to past changes or similar situations, you can predict how they might react to future changes

- Ongoing observation allows you to see what works and what doesn't in real-time, enabling continuous improvement of your change management strategies.

- Close observation helps in identifying potential risks associated with stakeholder reactions.

- As Robert Mckee said, every person/character live in three spheres, one inside the other. A self within a self within a self. The innermost sphere churns with the unsayable; the middle sphere restrains the unsaid; the outer sphere releases the said. In order the watch a stakeholder closely, we need to pay attention to the three spheres.

XV. Satisfy stakeholders

Story: A beautiful story — but above all, a credible One

It was a high-stakes project — the kind that, if successful, echoes through the halls of progress long after it's done. The technology? Cutting-edge. The supplier? A multinational powerhouse, deeply rooted in the global innovation landscape. The stakes were twofold: mastering the technology, yes — but even more so, earning the trust of a steering committee chairman known for his uncompromising standards.

This chairman wasn't one to be swayed by polished reports or flowery speeches. He verified everything himself, dug into the numbers, and challenged viewpoints. He never settled for easy consensus — he actively sought out blind spots, dissenting voices, and points of friction. Because he knew that's often where the truth hides. Demanding? Absolutely. But also, deeply fair. Suppliers feared him. Some even labeled him ill-intentioned — probably because he pushed them out of their comfort zones. Working with him meant being placed under a microscope — and yes, sometimes, it stung.

As is often the case with high-pressure projects, the initial deliverables arrived... late. The project's buffer was vanishing rapidly, and the looming threat of penalties hung overhead like the sword of Damocles. The multinational, keen on protecting its brand, had passed on other global opportunities to focus fully on this one. A bold gamble — now dangerously close to turning into a costly misstep.

Hamza, for his part, was walking a tightrope. Every step mattered. On one hand, he knew this project — the first of its kind in the MENA region — could launch his career to new heights. On the other, failure wouldn't just be a setback. It might be the end of his story at this company. He carried a double burden: success for the multinational... and success for himself.

Then came the long-dreaded day of the steering committee meeting. Seated across from him were the multinational's team — one of their CEOs included. But to Hamza's surprise, before any discussion of deliverables began, someone stood up... and told a story.

It was the story of a man — a senior expert — whose career had largely been shaped at NASA. He had worked alongside world-class minds, led complex projects across the globe, and earned the kind of reputation that made him fiercely protective of his name.

He refused to have it associated with anything subpar. On this project, he had gone above and beyond — not out of obligation, but out of passion. He'd found in it exactly what he was looking for: a challenge. What's more, the outcomes of the project had helped his team refine their own methodology. The results, he said, deserved to be published in leading journals.

And then, with a sincere smile, he added, "We'd be honored to work with you again."

Hamza was stunned. But what truly struck him was the chairman's reaction. For the first time, the exchange wasn't tense. It was clear, open, generous. They talked tech, vision, potential. They weren't hunting for errors anymore — they were mapping out a future.

After the meeting, the chairman — once thought unyielding — made an unexpected move: he asked Hamza to check the expert's credentials. Then, with deliberate weight, he asked,

"How can we build a long-term partnership with this company?"

Validating the current deliverables? That had become just a milestone in a far greater story.

From that day on, Hamza learned a priceless lesson: The real lever of transformation is the story you tell. Not to embellish the truth — but to give effort its rightful weight. Since then, before every strategic meeting, every high-stakes presentation, Hamza begins with a story. A beautiful story.But most importantly: a credible one.

And you?

You've likely faced demanding stakeholders too. You've put in the work, no doubt. But have you taken the time to tell the story behind your effort?

Not to convince. To make them feel. And if Hamza's story inspired you… maybe it's time to start telling your own.

How to satisfy stakeholders

"…every high-stakes presentation, Hamza begins with a story. A beautiful story.But most importantly: a credible one." That is a great lesson from HAMZA story.

Fleeting satisfaction is like a flash fire. What truly matters is what lasts. What binds. What endures. And what endures is trust. But trust doesn't fall from the sky. It's built — slowly, patiently — stone by stone. And those stones are credibility and consistency.

For a bond to hold, you must respect the other's intelligence. Never talk down to them. Never sell them empty promises. Because a stakeholder is not a passive observer — they are a clear-eyed actor, attuned to the disconnect between words and actions. That's why a narrative is only credible if it breathes reality. It must be grounded in tangible facts, in decisions that make sense, in actions that carry meaning. No need for spectacle — just sincerity. Storytelling isn't about seduction. It's about alignment. About making the project's story resonate with the expectations of those who believe in it — and even those who don't yet. Because in the end, to satisfy isn't to persuade. It's to inspire trust — again and again.

The best way to satisfy a stakeholder is to highlight the value of the deliverable or service provided to them. One effective approach is to create a narrative around it. There are three methods to craft such a story:

- Detail the efforts put into creating the deliverable or service.

- Compare the deliverable or service to similar ones in the market.

- Discuss the potential benefits or the actual benefits derived from the deliverable or service.

To effectively satisfy a stakeholder, it's crucial to emphasize the value of the deliverable or service. Crafting a compelling narrative around it can be a powerful method. Here's a detailed breakdown of the three strategies to create such a story:

Fig.13 Satisfy stakeholders

Detail the efforts put into creating the deliverable or service.

Elaborate on the meticulous planning, the expertise involved, and the challenges overcome during the development process. This narrative should highlight the dedication and innovation of the team, showcasing the technical skills, resource management, and problem-solving capabilities that were necessary to bring the project to fruition. By appreciating the complexity and effort invested, stakeholders can understand the quality and reliability of the deliverable or service.

Elaborate on the meticulous planning, the expertise involved, and the challenges overcome during the development process. This narrative should highlight the dedication and innovation of the team, showcasing the technical skills, resource management, and problem-solving capabilities that were necessary to bring the project to fruition. By appreciating the complexity and effort invested, stakeholders can understand the quality and reliability of the deliverable or service.

Team Expertise and Collaboration. Highlight the qualifications and experience of the team members involved in the project. Discuss how their unique skills were essential in different stages of the project, from initial concept through to execution. Emphasize the collaborative efforts, such as cross-functional teamwork and partnership with external experts, which were pivotal in overcoming technical challenges and achieving the project goals.

Planning and Resource Allocation: Describe the thorough planning process that underpinned the project. Include details on how resources were meticulously allocated to ensure maximum efficiency and effectiveness. Explain any adaptive strategies that were employed to respond to unexpected challenges or changes in project scope, showcasing the project management acumen of the team.

Innovation and Problem Solving. Detail the innovative approaches used in the project, whether they were technological innovations, novel applications of existing technologies, or creative problem-solving techniques. Discuss specific instances where the team had to think outside the box to overcome obstacles or to improve the project's outcome significantly.

Quality Assurance and Attention to Detail. Explain the measures taken to ensure the highest quality in the final deliverable or service. This might include quality control processes, testing phases, and any standards or best practices that were adhered to throughout the project lifecycle. Highlight how attention to detail was maintained to ensure that all aspects of the project met or exceeded the rigorous standards expected by stakeholders.

Milestones and Project Management Techniques. Outline the key milestones reached during the project and how these were integral to tracking progress and maintaining momentum. Discuss the project management methodologies employed (e.g., Agile, Lean, Waterfall) and how these facilitated effective project control and delivery within the desired timelines.

Emotional Engagement: Finally, don't underestimate the power of emotional engagement in your narrative. Share anecdotes or quotes from team members about their dedication, the challenges faced, and their pride in the accomplishments. This human element can make the narrative more relatable and compelling, reinforcing the stakeholder's confidence in the team's commitment to delivering excellence.

Compare the deliverable or service to similar ones in the market

Position your deliverable or service by contrasting it with competitors' offerings. This comparison can focus on superior features, enhanced efficiency, better cost-effectiveness, improved sustainability, or any other attributes that distinguish it in the marketplace. Provide specific examples or metrics that underscore these advantages, such as performance benchmarks, user testimonials, or market share data. This context helps stakeholders see the competitive edge and strategic value of choosing your deliverable or service.

Benchmarking Against Industry Standards:Start by identifying the industry standards or common benchmarks relevant to your deliverable or service. Explain how your offering meets or exceeds these standards, providing data or metrics that substantiate these claims. This could include performance metrics, durability tests, efficiency ratings, or user satisfaction scores. By aligning your deliverable with recognized standards, you provide a baseline for comparison that reassures stakeholders of its quality and reliability.

Feature-by-Feature Comparison: Create a detailed comparison of key features between your deliverable and its closest competitors. This can be presented in a tabular format where you list features such as usability, functionality, scalability, and support alongside each competitor for a direct comparison. Highlight features where your deliverable excels, and discuss the implications of these advantages for the stakeholder, such as increased productivity, reduced costs, or better user experience.

Cost Effectiveness and ROI: Discuss the cost-effectiveness of your deliverable or service compared to others. This involves not just the upfront costs but also the long-term value it offers. Illustrate potential savings over time, whether through lower maintenance requirements, higher durability, or more efficient performance. Include testimonials or case studies that demonstrate realized savings or ROI from customers who have switched from competitors' products or services.

Technological Advancements: Highlight any technological advancements that distinguish your deliverable from others on the market. This might involve the use of newer technologies, better integration capabilities, or innovations that enhance performance. Explain how these technological enhancements translate into real-world benefits for users, such as time savings, error reduction, or enhanced data security.

Market Position and User Feedback: Refer to market research or user feedback to demonstrate how your deliverable is perceived in the market compared to others. Positive reviews, high user ratings, and awards or recognitions can serve as strong endorsements of your deliverable's superiority. Discuss any surveys, user testimonials, or third-party reviews that reflect the satisfaction of users with your product or service, focusing on aspects that users have pointed out as particularly beneficial or superior.

Environmental and Social Impact: If applicable, include a discussion of the environmental or social impact of your deliverable. This is particularly relevant in today's market where consumers and businesses are increasingly making decisions based on sustainability and corporate social responsibility. Detail how your product reduces environmental impact, contributes to social causes, or improves adherence to ethical practices compared to competitors.

By thoroughly detailing these points, you not only underscore the unique attributes and advantages of your deliverable or service but also equip stakeholders with the information they need to make an informed decision, recognizing the distinct value your offering provides over the competition.

Discuss the potential benefits or the actual benefits derived from the deliverable or service.

Articulate the tangible and intangible benefits that the stakeholder can expect. This could include immediate gains like cost savings and efficiency improvements, as well as long-term benefits such as scalability, supportability, and alignment with broader business goals or regulatory compliance. If the deliverable or service has been in use, cite case studies or real-world outcomes that demonstrate its impact. By connecting the deliverable to concrete results, stakeholders can visualize the return on investment and the strategic importance of the deliverable in their operations or business landscape.

you can provide a comprehensive view of how it positively impacts the stakeholder. This part of the narrative should emphasize both immediate and long-term benefits, offering concrete examples and quantifiable outcomes where possible:

Immediate Operational Benefits: Detail the direct benefits that the deliverable or service offers immediately upon implementation. This could include improvements in efficiency, speed, or quality of operations. For instance, if the deliverable is a new software tool, you might discuss how it automates previously manual tasks, reduces processing times, or minimizes errors. Provide specific metrics that quantify these improvements, such as percentage reductions in time or increases in output.

Strategic Advantages: Explore how the deliverable aligns with and supports the broader strategic goals of the organization. Whether it's enhancing competitive advantage, entering new markets, or improving customer satisfaction, show how this deliverable serves as a key enabler. For example, if the service includes customer support, discuss how it increases customer loyalty and retention by providing reliable, 24/7 assistance.

Cost Savings and Financial Impact: Elaborate on how the deliverable or service leads to cost savings. This could be through more efficient resource use, lower maintenance costs, or reduced need for replacements. Illustrate these savings with scenarios or case studies that demonstrate the financial impact over time. If available, use data from existing users who have reported reduced costs due to the adoption of your deliverable.

Scalability and Future Proofing: Discuss the scalability of the deliverable and how it can grow with the stakeholder's needs. This is crucial for stakeholders to understand how the investment will continue to pay off as their operations expand or evolve. Explain any modular features or upgradable options that allow the deliverable to adapt to future demands without requiring a complete overhaul.

Enhanced Compliance and Risk Management: If relevant, highlight how the deliverable helps in compliance with industry regulations and reduces risk. Provide examples of how it addresses specific regulatory requirements or mitigates risks associated with non-compliance. This could include data protection features in software or safety mechanisms in machinery that help avoid accidents and legal issues.

Long-term Reliability and Support: Assure stakeholders of the long-term reliability and support available with the deliverable. Discuss the support structures in place, such as customer service teams, technical support, and warranty programs. Highlight any testimonials or feedback from long-term users that underscore the dependability and customer satisfaction associated with the deliverable.

Enhancing Reputation and Market Perception: Finally, consider how the deliverable or service can enhance the stakeholder's reputation. This might be through association with cutting-edge technology, leadership in sustainability, or superior customer service. Discuss how this improved perception can open new business opportunities, attract talent, or increase market share.

By detailing these benefits, you help stakeholders visualize the practical and strategic value of the deliverable or service, reinforcing their decision-making process with clear, impactful reasons why your offering stands out as the optimal choice.

By expanding on these points, the narrative becomes not just informative but also persuasive, aligning the stakeholders' expectations with the demonstrated value of the deliverable or service.

How to adapt and create your own story

Insightful points	Your story
Think about a key stakeholder who you have to satisfy.	•
Think about a great success of you, a team or team member who manage this issue by highlighting the value of the deliverable or service provided to them.	•
Have you used the effort put into creating the deliverable or service.	•
Have you compared the deliverable or service to similar ones in the market.	•
Have you discussed the potential benefits or the actual benefits derived from the deliverable or service.	•
Reflect on what said above. What were the hows and whys that led to the success.	•
Describe and amplify how actions and decisions were made during that experience, before and after.	•
What were the lesson learned about how to satisfy stakeholders.	•
Construct a story based on the points above	•
Share it with someone to give you feedback.	•

Takeaways

The best way to satisfy a stakeholder is to highlight the value of the deliverable or service provided to them. One effective approach is to create a narrative around it. There are three methods to craft such a story:

- Detail the efforts put into creating the deliverable or service.

- Compare the deliverable or service to similar ones in the market.

- Discuss the potential benefits or the actual benefits derived from the deliverable or service.

XVI. Prepare the engagement ground

Story: What is his story?

"What is his story?" This question, posed years earlier during a strategic meeting, still haunted Rachid. It dated back to a distant morning when, as a young and passionate project manager, his former director had inquired about the background of a future partner. Rachid, at a loss for words, had been plunged into a deep reflection. The partner in question was a potential supplier, tasked with introducing revolutionary technology for detailed mapping of plant species, promising significant advancements in predicting agricultural production.

At that time, the digital universe had not yet unveiled its vast networks of information. Data was primarily the privilege of large multinationals, and Rachid faced a glaring lack of information. Under pressure from his director, who had given him a 24-hour deadline, he embarked on a frantic quest for information, reaching out to colleagues from various companies who had previously collaborated with this supplier.

Rachid had gathered data on shareholders, revenue, the history of projects, and their geographic locations. However, the next day, his director sharply remarked, "You've gathered everything but the essence. A story is not just a series of facts; it's a fabric of decisions and sequential actions. How can you consider closely collaborating with a partner without understanding their decision-making processes?"

Resuming his investigation, Rachid refined his questions to identify the stakes and decision-making methodologies of the supplier. He discovered that the major challenge for the supplier was to use this project as a springboard to test their new technology and consider regional expansion. Their decisions prioritized project diversity and relegated financial considerations to the background.

Armed with these new insights, Rachid was able to convince his director not to reduce the project to a mere laboratory test and to integrate a technology transfer component, allowing them to benefit from the future evolution of the technology. The supplier, convinced, accepted these recommendations without reservation.

Since this learning experience, Rachid has made it a practice to weave a story for each stakeholder. Now a director himself, he approves no project without a deep understanding of the narratives of key actors. This narrative approach, inspired by his experience, has not only enriched his understanding of project dynamics but also strengthened his collaboration strategies.

And you, in the projects you have been involved in, have you constructed narratives profiling your stakeholders? What strengths have you identified, and how, inspired by Rachid's experience, could you improve your approach?

How to prepare the ground for watching Key stakeholder

True engagement doesn't start with a name on a stakeholder map. It starts long before that. It begins in the shadows of silent decisions, where the invisible threads of what drives a person are quietly woven. Observing a stakeholder isn't just about collecting data. It's about listening to them breathe through their choices. It's about tracing, between the lines, the mental path that leads them to say yes, no, or nothing at all.

Because every decision is a chapter. And every chapter reveals a protagonist searching for alignment, for meaning, for impact. So why not help write that story with them? Not by manipulating the narrative, but by illuminating it—by becoming, if only for a moment, the quiet co-author of their journey. In this context, storytelling isn't about embellishment. It's about preparing the ground. It's about laying the first stones of a fertile alliance, where every word, every gesture, every silence matters.

Engaging stakeholders effectively is crucial for the success of any project or initiative. To do this, understanding their decision-making process, information priorities, interpretative frameworks, response to challenges, and risk tolerance is essential. Here's a detailed exploration of each of these elements.

Fig. 14 Prepare the engagement ground

How the Stakeholder Makes Decisions.Why: Knowing how a stakeholder makes decisions helps in tailoring communication and proposals that align with their decision-making style. This can lead to more effective persuasion and successful stakeholder management. Observe past decisions, ask direct questions during meetings, and gather insights from peers or reports who have interacted with the stakeholder. Understanding whether their approach is data-driven, consensus-based, intuitive, or authority-driven will influence how you present information and proposals to them. Tailoring your approach based on the stakeholder's decision-making style can lead to faster and more favorable decisions, fostering a stronger relationship and smoother project execution.

What is the Most Relevant Information to Decision Making. Stakeholders are often busy and need to sift through a lot of information. Identifying what information is most relevant to them ensures that communications are concise and impactful. Analyze which types of information the stakeholder has prioritized in the past. This can be achieved by reviewing the documents they frequently reference, the questions they typically ask, or by directly inquiring about their preferences. By focusing on relevant information, you can increase the effectiveness of your communications, making it easier for stakeholders to make informed decisions quickly, which is especially crucial in fast-paced environments.

The Hypotheses That Frame the Interpretation of Gathered Information. Stakeholders often have preconceived notions or hypotheses that influence how they interpret information. Understanding these can help in framing your messages in a way that resonates with their existing beliefs or challenges them effectively. Listen carefully to the stakeholder's queries and assertions in meetings to identify underlying assumptions. Engage in discussions that explore these hypotheses directly or indirectly to clarify and challenge them when necessary. Addressing and aligning with their interpretive frameworks can lead to more persuasive arguments and a higher likelihood of stakeholder buy-in, as it ensures that your proposals fit within their worldview or convincingly expand it.

How the Stakeholder Responds to Challenges: Why: Understanding a stakeholder's response to challenges helps in anticipating their needs and reactions in crisis situations, allowing for better support and more tailored solutions. Observe their past behavior in difficult situations, note their strategies in overcoming obstacles, and consider feedback from others who have seen them under pressure. This knowledge allows you to approach the stakeholder with solutions and support that align with their approach to problems, thereby enhancing trust and collaboration.

What is the Stakeholder's Tolerance to Risk. A stakeholder's risk tolerance affects their willingness to engage in new or innovative endeavors. Knowing this can guide how you propose projects and manage potential concerns. Review past initiatives they have approved or rejected and discuss hypothetical scenarios to gauge their risk appetite. This can be supplemented by feedback from colleagues or direct dialogue. Understanding risk tolerance enables you to tailor project proposals to match the stakeholder's comfort level, potentially increasing the chances of approval and avoiding proposals that are likely to be rejected due to perceived risks.

By closely monitoring and understanding these aspects of stakeholder behavior, you can craft more effective engagement strategies that foster positive relationships and facilitate successful project outcomes.

But more specifically, in order to construct the stakeholder story we need to build in on what is below:

Effectively monitoring key stakeholders requires a deep understanding of their motivations, actions, and the broader impact of their involvement in a project. These factors are interconnected, influencing each other in a dynamic cycle. Here's a breakdown of the key aspects to watch and how they influence one another:

What is the Stake? (Positive or Negative Impact on the Stakeholder). stakeholders engage based on their perceived benefits or risks associated with the project. Their stake may be financial, reputational, operational, or strategic. Identify what the stakeholder stands to gain or lose — this will dictate their level of involvement and influence. For example, a government regulator may have a compliance-driven stake, while an investor may focus on profitability and return on investment. The more significant the stake, the higher the likelihood of active engagement. Stakeholders with high stakes may exert strong influence over decision-making, project priorities, or even delays if their concerns are not addressed.

What is the Stakeholder's Desire? A stakeholder's desires often go beyond just their stake. While their stake reflects objective factors (profit, risk, power), their desires can include subjective goals such as career advancement, public recognition, or ideological alignment with the project's mission. Understanding both explicit desires (what they say) and implicit desires (what they truly want but may not articulate) is crucial. This can be assessed through direct discussions, past behaviors, and public statements. A stakeholder whose desires align with the project's goals will likely be a strong advocate. Conversely, if their desires conflict with the project's direction, they may become an obstacle or even mobilize opposition.

Based on Stake & Desire, the Stakeholder Takes Action. Stakeholders do not remain passive—they act based on their stakes and desires. Their actions can either facilitate or hinder project progress. Observe their communication, lobbying efforts, decision-making patterns, and influence over other stakeholders. Are they investing resources, voicing support, raising concerns, or creating roadblocks? The nature of their action—whether cooperative or obstructive—will determine the immediate challenges or opportunities for project management. Recognizing this early allows for proactive engagement.

What is the Result of the Action Taken? Actions lead to tangible consequences, which can validate or challenge the stakeholder's expectations. This affects future stakeholder behavior. Measure the impact of their action—did it achieve the intended outcome? Did it lead to a project acceleration, policy change, or resource allocation? If the action achieves the stakeholder's intended goal, they may continue or intensify similar actions. If not, they may shift tactics, escalate their involvement, or disengage.

What is the Gap Between Expectation and Result? A mismatch between expectations and reality can cause frustration, disappointment, or increased aggression from stakeholders. Compare what the stakeholder anticipated versus what actually happened. This gap is often a driver for renegotiation, conflict, or even withdrawal. If expectations are exceeded: Stakeholders become stronger allies, possibly increasing their investment or advocacy. If expectations are unmet: The stakeholder may escalate concerns, demand changes, or reduce support.

How Do Other Stakeholders React? No stakeholder exists in isolation—others are always watching. Stakeholder actions influence the behavior of other key players in the project ecosystem. Assess whether other stakeholders rally behind, oppose, or remain neutral in response to an action. For example, if a key sponsor withdraws support, will others follow? If a government agency enforces stricter regulations, will other regulatory bodies adopt similar measures? A positive ripple effect (support grows) can accelerate project momentum. A negative ripple effect (opposition builds) can lead to widespread resistance, project delays, or cancellations.

What is the Risk? Every stakeholder action and reaction introduce potential risks, including financial, operational, political, and reputational risks.Identify risks related to:

- Escalation of opposition
- Legal and regulatory intervention
- Financial withdrawal
- Supply chain disruptions
- Negative public perception

Understanding the risk allows for proactive risk mitigation strategies, such as contingency planning, negotiation, or strategic alliances.

What is the Next Action Based on the Above Factors? Stakeholder engagement is an ongoing process that requires continuous adaptation based on evolving dynamics. According to the gap between results and expectations, the risk appetite of the stakeholder, he will make decision and take the next action until he is satisfied or convinced otherwise.

By systematically monitoring these factors, project managers and leaders can anticipate challenges, leverage opportunities, and engage stakeholders in a way that maximizes project success.

How to adapt and create your own story

Insightful points	Your story
Think about a key stakeholder who you have to satisfy, to watch or just to keep informed.	•
Think about a context when you collect information about: their decision-making process, information priorities, interpretative frameworks, response to challenges, and risk tolerance.	•
Think about how all the information or part of it has helped you, team or team member to succeed, in engaging a key stakeholder.	•
Reflect on what said above. What were the hows and whys that led to the success.	•
Describe and amplify how actions and decisions were made during that experience, before and after.	•
What were the lesson learned about how to engage stakeholders.	•
Construct a story based on the points above	•
Share it with someone to give you feedback.	•

Takeaways

In order to engage a stakeholder by using a storytelling, you need prepare the ground for it. It means you have to know his/her story. To do so, you need to collect information about:

- His/her decision-making process;
- His/her information priorities;
- His/her interpretative frameworks;
- How he/she responses to challenges;
- What is his/her risk tolerance.

XVII.   Making sense out of complexity

Story: China Success Story (green energy)

During the 1980s, at the height of the Cold War, the world was marked by palpable geopolitical tension between the superpowers of the East and West. It was a period when the global economy began to take shape around globalization, driven by the development of trade and international investments. At the same time, newly industrialized economies in Asia were emerging, opening pathways to global markets and thus facilitating manufacturing and technology transfer from developed nations. However, this landscape was also darkened by political instability in various regions and increased protectionism in developed countries, facing technological shifts that threatened to place China at a competitive disadvantage. Despite an abundant workforce, the Chinese economy suffered from significant shortcomings such as underdeveloped infrastructure, outdated technology, and limited access to international markets. In response to these challenges, the Chinese government resolutely embarked on a policy of economic reforms and openness, establishing special economic zones to attract foreign investors and implementing market reforms in agricultural and industrial sectors.

The 1990s, marking the end of the Cold War and significant expansion of the European Union, witnessed rapid advancements in information and communication technologies. These new conditions opened up increased global economic integration opportunities for China, particularly through trade and investment. Access to advanced technologies and a growing demand for consumer goods spurred rapid industrialization. Leveraging its abundant and increasingly skilled workforce, China was able to establish a thriving export market[1]. It adopted policies that favored direct foreign investment and focused on technological upgrades and skill development while enhancing its infrastructure to produce high-value-added goods. By the end of this decade, China positioned itself as the world leader in the production of rare earths[2], controlling a substantial portion of the global market thanks to its competitive production costs and lenient environmental regulations.

The 2000s were characterized by trade imbalances and rising protectionism, amid environmental challenges exacerbated by resource tensions. China, with a robust manufacturing base and expanding technology, as well as a growing middle class boosting domestic consumption, distinguished itself by strengthening its leadership in the manufacturing sector. To support this growth and meet the needs of a developing middle class, the government ramped up investments in urbanization and national infrastructure, thus fostering the expansion of the domestic market. However, this industrial expansion significantly impacted the environment in China's major cities. Investing in high-speed rail technologies and promoting sustainable development, China launched the Renewable Energy Law in 2005 [3], aiming to diversify its energy mix and reduce its reliance on imported fossil fuels while improving urban life quality.

The 2010s saw the rise of artificial intelligence and big data technologies. Aware of the stakes of climate change, China reinforced its leadership in renewable energies and technologies, supported by a government policy that favored innovation and global connectivity, notably through the "Belt and Road" initiative [4]. In 2015, it launched the "Made in China 2025" initiative to enhance the quality of its manufactured products, thus demonstrating its determination to maintain its lead in a post-COVID world marked by accelerated digital transformation and persistent geopolitical tensions. Despite economic uncertainties and the vulnerability of the global supply chain, the resilience of the Chinese economy in manufacturing and the strength of its supply chains underline a skillfully orchestrated strategy to navigate the tumults of a changing global order.

How to make sense off all?

A decision is never born in isolation. It takes root in a complex soil, nourished by the spirit of the times, swept by opposing winds — from the industry, the economy, the social climate, and geopolitical tensions. In other words: every decision is a child of its era, its environment, and the dominant narratives that shape them. Every field, every domain of activity, is steeped in stories — stories we share, repeat, and eventually come to believe. These narratives are the invisible compasses guiding the players involved: they direct without forcing, influence without noise, permeate without pressure. So, to engage a stakeholder is first to recognize the story they're living in. It's about grasping the words that drive them, the images that comfort them, the fears they keep silent. And more importantly, it's about offering a narrative that resonates — one that stays rooted in reality, yet opens up a horizon. In a world in flux, storytelling is not a luxury. It's a lever. A compass. An invitation to make sense of things — together. Because it's precisely within this subtle alignment of context, narrative, and action that true engagement is born.

In Kos, people are feeling desperate and are struggling to find clarity amidst the overwhelming confusion that permeates our world—a world that, paradoxically, should be more comprehensible than ever. Despite the unprecedented levels of communication, we experience today, this abundance of information often leads to greater confusion rather than enhanced understanding. In this environment, clarity becomes a precious commodity.

Fig. 15 Making sense of all

Storytelling emerges as a powerful tool in such times, serving not just as a method of communication but as a framework for making sense of the chaos. Good storytelling can cut through the noise and confusion by presenting information in a manner that is not only accessible but also resonant on a human level. It allows leaders to weave facts into narratives that are meaningful and compelling, helping people to see beyond the data and understand the broader context.

Leaders who master the art of storytelling can effectively guide their communities or organizations by creating narratives that clarify their visions and rally support. These stories can illuminate paths through the darkness of uncertainty, providing the sense-making framework necessary for people to evaluate their circumstances and make informed decisions. In this way, storytelling is not just about entertainment or engagement but becomes a strategic tool in leadership, crucial for driving action and change.

As we consider the role of leaders in turbulent times, their ability to craft and communicate clear, persuasive stories is paramount. These narratives become the lens through which chaos is interpreted and understood, transforming confusion into clarity and despair into direction. By fostering a culture where storytelling is harnessed to distill complex issues into understandable and actionable messages, leaders can ensure that their guidance is not only heard but followed, steering their communities toward coherence and purpose in an often-disordered world.

As a first step gather information about hard/physical components

Gathering Comprehensive Information: Start by collecting data across four critical areas. Sector Overview: Understand the broader industry or sector dynamics, including market trends, key players, and regulatory environment. Organization-Specific Details: Focus on the internal aspects of the organization such as culture, operational processes, and strategic objectives. Infrastructure Insights: Examine the physical and IT infrastructure that supports the organization, noting any limitations or advantages they present. Technological Landscape: Keep abreast of the technological tools and platforms the organization uses, and how they integrate with or enhance operational capabilities.

For each the component specified above we need to Identify key events that have significantly impacted the sector or organization, both positively and negatively. To Detect and analyze ongoing trends that could influence future strategies and operations. And to utilize a systems thinking perspective to uncover deep structural issues within the organization or sector. This involves looking at the interconnections and potential systemic challenges that might not be immediately obvious. When faced with insufficient information, it's crucial to develop theoretical models of the system. This involves hypothesizing how different components of the organization or sector interact based on the available data.

These steps, when performed systematically, enhance the ability of leaders to make informed decisions. By structuring the information narrative clearly, storytelling not only clarifies the present situation but also helps in predicting and shaping future scenarios. However, the next step and the most important one is to pay attention to what we could call information about soft or immaterial components like Believes, hypothesis and Prevailing narratives.

As a second step gather information about soft/immaterial components

Another critical step involves delving into the softer, less tangible aspects of the environment:

Beliefs: Understanding the underlying beliefs of a community or organization is crucial. These are the foundational values and assumptions that influence behavior and decision-making processes. Mapping out these beliefs helps in anticipating how groups might respond to different scenarios, which is invaluable for strategic planning.

Understanding the prevailing beliefs of individuals and groups within the context is crucial. Beliefs influence how information is processed and which actions are considered acceptable or rejected. Leaders must grasp these underlying beliefs to predict responses to policies or initiatives, tailor communications effectively, and foster an environment of mutual understanding and cooperation.

Hypotheses: Formulating hypotheses based on observed data and beliefs can guide further inquiry and experimentation. These educated guesses allow leaders to explore potential outcomes and plan interventions. Hypotheses should be continuously tested and refined with new information, ensuring that strategies remain relevant and effective. Formulating hypotheses involves making educated guesses based on available information. This step is critical in decision-making as it allows leaders to anticipate potential outcomes and assess various scenarios before committing to a course of action. Hypotheses act as a bridge between the known and the unknown, guiding leaders in resource allocation, strategy development, and contingency planning.

Prevailing Narratives: Identifying the dominant narratives within the community or organization is vital. These narratives shape how people perceive their environment and dictate the collective response to challenges. Leaders need to understand these narratives to effectively communicate and implement change. By crafting messages that resonate with these prevailing stories, leaders can foster greater alignment and motivate action towards common goals. The stories that are widely accepted and circulated within a community or organization shape the social and cultural context of decision-making. These narratives can significantly influence public opinion and organizational culture, steering the direction of collective action. Leaders need to be aware of these narratives to effectively communicate their decisions, align their actions with public sentiments, or challenge and change outdated or harmful narratives.

By focusing on these immaterial components — beliefs, hypotheses, and narratives — leaders can gain deeper insights into the motivations and behaviors of their constituents. This understanding is critical for crafting strategies that are not only logical but also resonate deeply with the community's values and experiences.

As the third step what are the Main Actors/characters.

A critical step in constructing such a narrative is gathering information about the main actors or key stakeholders in the system. Understanding these players provides insight into past, present, and future dynamics, allowing for a more accurate and compelling storyline about the environment as a whole.

Identifying Main Actors/Stakeholders: Determine who the key players are within the sector or issue at hand. This includes both internal and external stakeholders ranging from management, employees, customers, suppliers, regulators, and the local community.

Understanding Their Needs/Desires: Assess what each stakeholder wants to achieve or what drives their engagement with the organization or community. Understanding these motivations is critical for addressing their concerns and harnessing their support.

Analyzing Past Decisions: Look into the significant decisions these stakeholders have made in the past. This helps in understanding their decision-making patterns, priorities, and the outcomes of their choices.

Predicting Future Decisions: Based on their past behavior and current trends, predict possible future decisions they might make. This foresight can be instrumental in strategic planning and risk management.

Decision-Making Processes: Examine how these stakeholders make their decisions. Are they data-driven, consensus-oriented, or do they rely on a few key opinions? Understanding this process helps in crafting messages and strategies that resonate with their decision-making styles.

Successful Stories of Key Stakeholders: Identify the most successful outcomes for these stakeholders. Analyzing these success stories can provide valuable insights into what works well and how similar results can be replicated or adapted in current scenarios.

Challenges Faced in the Past: Review the major challenges these stakeholders have encountered previously. This examination not only highlights their areas of vulnerability but also the resilience and adaptability they have shown over time.

Future Challenges: Anticipate potential challenges that could impact these stakeholders moving forward. This foresight is essential for developing strategies that help mitigate risks and leverage opportunities.

By thoroughly understanding these aspects, leaders can craft more effective strategies that are closely aligned with the needs and behaviors of key stakeholders. This approach not only aids in immediate decision-making but also in long-term strategic planning, ensuring responses are proactive rather than reactive.

Understanding these factors allows us to build a structured and compelling narrative. Here's how:

Identify the Main Conflict or Challenge: A strong story needs a central issue. Is it a clash between government policy and corporate interests? A struggle for sustainability in a profit-driven world? A fight for technological dominance?

Create Stakeholder Perspectives: Each stakeholder has a voice in the story. Their motivations, decisions, and past experiences shape how they respond to events.

Establish a Timeline: How did we get here? What major events shaped the current situation? What turning points were critical?

Analyze Power Dynamics: Who has the most influence? Who is struggling? What alliances or conflicts are emerging?

Develop a Vision for the Future: What are the possible outcomes? Is there a clear trajectory toward progress or crisis? What actions can be taken to alter the course?

In an era where information overload creates more confusion than clarity, storytelling serves as a bridge between complexity and understanding. By systematically analyzing key stakeholders—who they are, what they need, how they decide, and what challenges they face—we construct a narrative that not only explains the present but also anticipates the future. Leaders who master this approach can make better decisions, drive meaningful action.

Making sense of all: the green energy

China's journey in the realm of green energy unfolds as an exemplary saga, a model worth scrutinizing to distill its essence and extract vital lessons. By meticulously shaping this narrative, we can structure information, imbue it with deep meaning, and derive crucial lessons. These lessons become the pillars of a strategic decision-making framework aimed at identifying win-win opportunities, the foundation of any successful stakeholder engagement.

In this narrative where ambition and caution intertwine, China's energy trajectory offers rich perspectives in win-win alliances, eloquently illustrating that moving towards greener horizons is not only an ecological imperative but also a lever for shared development. Far from being merely a chronicle, this story serves as an operational guide for any entity seeking sustainable transformation.

Every initiative must be structured on multiple levels, with crucial decisions based on carefully crafted hypotheses. These assumptions must encompass all available data on key sectors, ensuring a comprehensive approach to the value chain. Thus, decisions will maximize opportunities and minimize risks to achieve the desired benefits. Critical performance areas might include local assets, infrastructure and distribution capacity, alliances and coalitions, skills and expertise, market lessons, and a flexible and effective governance system.

- **Valuing Local Assets:** Every player should anchor themselves in value chains by identifying assets to leverage: critical mineral deposits to attract investors, vast areas suitable for solar or wind energy production, or the potential for green hydrogen extraction as the foundation for strategic partnerships. These resources, difficult to relocate and currently in high demand, have shown, especially during the COVID-19 pandemic, that they are best valued where they are found.

- **Developing Infrastructure and Distribution Capacity:** Transporting energy is a significant challenge. Renewable energies are expected to account for between 45% and 50% of global electricity production by 2030, and potentially 65% to 85% by 2050. Integrating these high levels requires significant upgrades to existing infrastructure. Access to the energy produced and the full potential of this opportunity depend on adequate infrastructure.

- **Establishing Partnerships and Coalitions:** Capitalizing on this vast opportunity requires close collaboration among diverse skills and capabilities across multiple companies and countries. No single actor, not even a country, possesses all the resources necessary to deliver green energy to the end consumer. It is therefore crucial to focus on one's core competencies and forge alliances with complementary partners.

- **Enhancing Skills and Abilities:** Technological uncertainty is high, and R&D efforts are ongoing. It is essential to engage in the development of specific skills to stay at the forefront of fundamental changes, such as energy density, cost, and material availability.

- **Quickly Leveraging Market Lessons:** Industries that consume green energy, such as the electric vehicle market, must be constantly monitored to identify trends and guide investment flows. Understanding market dynamics allows strategies to be adapted and effectively responds to new regulations or geopolitical changes.

- **Establishing an Agile and Effective Governance System:** In an uncertain and complex environment, having a governance system capable of making quick decisions is crucial. Former partners may become competitors and vice versa. Diversified and well-informed governance is essential for making informed and relevant decisions.

In this evolving ecosystem, decisions are generally made based on observed information. For example, China's recent decision to restrict the export of rare earths is a political maneuver that will influence the cost and availability of these materials, as well as the profitability analysis of related initiatives. This will also encourage global rare earth mining exploration. The next phase of orientation involves analyzing and synthesizing all information to quickly develop new hypotheses, followed by prompt decisions to take action. This continuous cycle ensures that the decision-making system remains flexible and effective, and initiatives remain resilient to change.

How to adapt and create your own story

Insightful points	Your story
Think about a context where you have been faced with complexity: lot of information to collect and interpret, lots of stakeholders to engage, decision that change all the time…	•
Think about the hard/soft information, how they lead to stakeholders' decision making?	•
What is or was the Main Conflict or Challenge? What were the main Stakeholder Perspectives? Analyze Power Dynamics	•
Is/was there a clear trajectory toward progress or crisis?	•
Reflect on what said above. What were the hows and whys that led to the progress or crisis.	•
Describe and amplify how actions and decisions are/were made in this context.	•
What are/were the lesson learned/could be learned about how to engage stakeholders.	•
Construct a story based on the points above	•
Share it with someone to give you feedback.	•

Takeaways

- o As a first step gather information about hard/physical components.
  - Sector dynamics, including market trends, key players, and regulatory environment.
  - Organization-Specific Details Focus on the internal aspects of the organization such as culture, operational processes, and strategic objectives.
  - Infrastructure Insights and accessibility.
  - Technological Landscape
- o As a second step gather information about soft/immaterial components
  - Beliefs
  - Hypotheses
  - Prevailing Narratives
- o As the third step what are the Main Actors/characters.
  - Understanding Their Needs/Desires:
  - Analyzing Past Decisions
  - Predicting Future Decisions
  - Decision-Making Processes

- Successful Stories of Key Stakeholders

- Challenges Faced in the Past

o Future Challenges

Understanding these factors allows us to build a structured and compelling narrative by:

o Identify the Main Conflict or Challenge

o Create Stakeholder Perspectives

o Analyze Power Dynamics

o Develop a Vision for the Future

o Is there a clear trajectory toward progress or crisis?

EPILOGUE: FELIX'S STORIES

Felix was no ordinary project manager. He was a sculptor of momentum, a guardian of detail, a weaver of true stories. Certified as a PMP, he had mastered the grammar of project control — but it was by speaking to hearts, not just dashboards, that he led his projects to excellence. To him, a project wasn't just a deliverable. It was a human odyssey. Every success, a living tapestry he knew how to bring to life. And through the power of honest storytelling and concrete wins, he climbed the ladder to become a project director in a global company.

But one day, the wind shifted. A new CEO stepped in — colder, more Cartesian. During a quarterly meeting, as Felix prepared to spotlight a flagship project through a carefully crafted narrative, the CEO cut him off. Silent at first. Then skeptical. Then ice-cold. From that day on, everything changed. What was once praised became a target for mockery. Even those Felix had mentored and inspired began to pull back. Until one day, a cutting phrase landed in a boardroom too small to contain that much ego:

"Stop telling us Felix's stories."

Storytelling was suddenly labeled populist. Leadership launched an official initiative to return to rational methods." The cruel irony? Felix was appointed to lead the initiative. The man of stories was now tasked with burying them. Those were dark days. Felix came close to resigning. Because it wasn't just stories, they were rejecting — it was his voice, his authenticity, his way of honoring journeys, efforts, and human connection. But the story — the real one — wasn't over.

Before a high-stakes meeting with an international partner, Felix took a quiet initiative. He wrote a powerful story — not about himself, but about the company. Its roots. Its storms. Its resilience. He didn't spotlight his role or his achievements. He let the organization shine — its leaders, past and present. Then, humbly, he handed the story to the CEO: "I think it would be more impactful if you were the one to tell it."

The CEO accepted, almost offhandedly. But the partner was moved. The story struck the right chord. It resonated. And in that moment, the CEO understood. A door cracked open. Curiosity was born. Felix sought no revenge, no recognition. He simply understood: a story, once shared, no longer belongs to the one who tells it. It becomes leverage. A bond. A beam of light. Storytelling isn't just a management tool — it's an organizational skill. It shouldn't be confined to project management — it should be seeded throughout the structure, from strategy to operations.

When a story is true, when it's offered — not imposed — it doesn't divide. It unites. And Felix no longer wanted to convince. He wanted to pass it on. So, others could tell their own stories. So that the energy of many could become shared momentum. So, you, reading this now — Have you thought about passing on what you've learned from storytelling, beyond your own projects? To whom could you hand the mic? Because sometimes, real courage isn't in telling the story. It's in letting it live through other voices. In the whole organization.

CONCLUSION

From Félix's story, we don't just learn about a man—we gain insight into our times. Félix, a project manager turned storyteller of odysseys, shows us that beyond Gantt charts and performance indicators, there lies another lever: the power of narrative. When wielded skillfully, storytelling isn't about embellishing action—it's about giving it meaning. It weaves through the five project management process groups like a subtle but potent thread: it inspires during initiation, unites in planning, engages during execution, soothes in monitoring, and preserves legacy in closure.

But the strength of a story doesn't lie solely in the voice that tells it. It also depends on the ear that listens, and the culture that welcomes it. Even the most beautiful stories fade in the cold hallways of deaf organizations. What Félix's story quietly teaches us is that the impact of storytelling relies less on the storyteller and more on the soil in which the words are planted. If the organizational environment doesn't recognize narrative as a tool for guidance, momentum wanes, words fall flat, and stories die before they can create shared meaning.

So, it's not enough to learn how to tell stories. Storytelling must be established as a living system, deeply rooted in the organization's culture. Not as a trend, but as a method. Not as decoration, but as structure. This requires a strategic approach: mapping stakeholders, tailoring stories to their expectations, training teams, creating storytelling rituals, and embedding collective memory into projects. In short, it means turning narrative into policy.

And that — now that is another journey. Another story. One made of quiet resistance and sudden breakthroughs. Of trial and error, failed narratives, and then stories that strike a chord, that mobilize, that transform. Because where we think of an organization as a machine, storytelling reminds us it is first and foremost a human community. And every community needs a story to believe in if it is to move forward. A story that is not written alone, but together.

REFERENCES

Part I:STORY POWER & STAKEHOLDERS ENGAGEMENT

Story power

1 : Platon, The republic.

2 : Raymond A. et all York University, Toronto, Ontario, Canada

b University of Toronto, Toronto, Ontario, Canada: Emotion and narrative fiction: Interactive influences before, during, and after reading.

3: Marina Kilintari et all
Brain_activation_profiles_during_kinesthetic_and_visual_imagery_An_fMRI_study

4: Paul J Zak : Why Inspiring Stories Make Us React: The Neuroscience of Narrative, PMCID: PMC4445577 PMID: 26034526

5: Antonio Damasio:Descartes' Error: Emotion, Reason, and the Human Brain

How to target stakeholders

1: Robert Dilts: Modeling With NLP

2: PMBOK V6: Project Management Institute (PMI)

3: Robert Mackee, STORY, substance, Structure, style, and the principles of screenwriting

4: Taiichi Ōno, Toyota Production System: beyond large-scale production, Productivity Press, (1988), (ISBN 0915299143)

5: Kvale, S., & Brinkmann, S. (2009). Interviews: Learning the craft of qualitative research interviewing (2nd ed.). Sage Publications, Inc.

6: Tim Brown, Change by Design: How Design Thinking Transforms Organizations and Inspires Innovation September 29, 2009

How to build the master idea to tell

1: John Truby: The anatomy of story

2: Robert Mackee, STORY, substance, Structure, style, and the principles of screenwriting

How to construct a story to tell

1: https://www.nobelprize.org/prizes/literature/1993/morrison/lecture/

2: Rizzolatti, G. and Craighero, L. (2004) The Mirror Neuron System. Annual Review of Neuroscience, 27, 169-192.

3: Robert Mackee, STORY, substance, Structure, style, and the principles of screenwriting

4: Burke, Kenneth.Literature as Equipment for Living 1973/1941. The Philosophy of Literary Form. Berkeley and Los Angeles: University of California Press. Pp. 293-304.

5: Joseph Campbell: The Hero with a Thousand Faces

PART II: PROJECT PROCESS AND STORYTELLING

Project processes groups and storytelling

1: PMBOK V6: Project Management Institute (PMI)

PART III: HOW TO TAILOR STORYTELLING TO TYPES OF STAKEHOLDERS

How to engage specific stakeholders

1: PMBOK V6: Project Management Institute (PMI)

Watch stakeholders closely

1: Robert Mackee, STORY, substance, Structure, style, and the principles of screenwriting

Making sense out of complexity

Making sense out of complexity

1:https://www.asil.org/insights/volume/3/issue/1/chinas-accession-wto

2:Energy technology perspectives 2023 (AIEA)

3:https://policy.asiapacificenergy.org/

4:https://en.wikipedia.org/wiki/Belt_and_Road_Initiative

ABOUT THE AUTHOR

Visionary CEO of HAMA CONSULTING, seasoned strategist, and certified expert in navigating complexity and driving meaningful change.

Holder of an MBA and a suite of prestigious certifications from the Project Management Institute — PGMP, PMP, PMI-RMP, PMI-ACP, PMI-PBA — with additional specialization from IDEO U in Design Thinking and Storytelling for Influence, leading change for success.

Licensed NLP Coach, passionate about unlocking human potential through transformative communication.

Former Director of Mining Asset Management & Promotion at ONHYM, where he led large-scale initiatives with national and international impact.

Author of *Le Muet* and *Trente et une nuits*, blending storytelling with societal insight.

With over 30 years of experience, he empowers organizations and leaders through training, coaching, and speaking engagements focused on program & project management, strategic influence, and narrative leadership.

Email: hamzaoui@hama-co.net

www.ingramcontent.com/pod-product-compliance
Lightning Source LLC
Chambersburg PA
CBHW020312160726
47992CB00004B/1499